Acting Edition

The Blank Theatre's Young Playwrights Festival 30th Anniversary Collection

The Legend of Caeneus
by Zander Pryor

stand. Up. HIT!
by Wyn Alyse Thomas

Gray Area
Simone Chaney

Dollface
by Jeremino Sutton

Droplets Pellets Bullets
by Isabel Beatriz Tongson

Under My Skin
by Disha Catt

The Legend of Caeneus © 2023 by Zander Pryor
stand. Up. HIT! © 2023 by Wyn Alyse Thomas
Gray Area © 2023 by Simone Chaney
Dollface © 2023 by Jeremino Sutton
Droplets Pellets Bullets © 2023 by Isabel Beatriz Tongson
Under My Skin © 2023 by Disha Catt
All Rights Reserved

THE BLANK THEATRE'S YOUNG PLAYWRIGHTS FESTIVAL 30TH ANNIVERSARY COLLECTION is fully protected under the copyright laws of the United States of America, the British Commonwealth, including Canada, and all member countries of the Berne Convention for the Protection of Literary and Artistic Works, the Universal Copyright Convention, and/or the World Trade Organization conforming to the Agreement on Trade Related Aspects of Intellectual Property Rights. All rights, including professional and amateur stage productions, recitation, lecturing, public reading, motion picture, radio broadcasting, television, online/digital production, and the rights of translation into foreign languages are strictly reserved.

ISBN 978-0-573-71045-2

www.concordtheatricals.com
www.concordtheatricals.co.uk

FOR PRODUCTION INQUIRIES

UNITED STATES AND CANADA
info@concordtheatricals.com
1-866-979-0447

UNITED KINGDOM AND EUROPE
licensing@concordtheatricals.co.uk
020-7054-7298

Each title is subject to availability from Concord Theatricals Corp., depending upon country of performance. Please be aware that *THE BLANK THEATRE'S YOUNG PLAYWRIGHTS FESTIVAL 30TH ANNIVERSARY COLLECTION* may not be licensed by Concord Theatricals Corp. in your territory. Professional and amateur producers should contact the nearest Concord Theatricals Corp. office or licensing partner to verify availability.

CAUTION: Professional and amateur producers are hereby warned that *THE BLANK THEATRE'S YOUNG PLAYWRIGHTS FESTIVAL 30TH ANNIVERSARY COLLECTION* is subject to a licensing fee. The purchase, renting, lending or use of this book does not constitute a license to perform this title(s), which license must be obtained from Concord Theatricals Corp. prior to any performance. Performance of this title(s) without a license is a violation of federal law and may subject the producer and/or presenter of such performances to civil penalties. Both amateurs and professionals considering a production are strongly advised to apply to the appropriate agent before starting rehearsals, advertising, or booking a theatre. A licensing fee must be paid whether the title(s) is presented for charity or gain and whether or not admission is charged. Professional/Stock licensing fees are quoted upon application to Concord Theatricals Corp.

This work is published by Samuel French, an imprint of Concord Theatricals Corp.

No one shall make any changes in this title(s) for the purpose of production. No part of this book may be reproduced, stored in a retrieval system, scanned, uploaded, or transmitted in any form, by any means, now known or yet to be invented, including mechanical, electronic, digital, photocopying, recording, videotaping, or otherwise, without the prior written permission of the publisher. No one shall share this title(s), or any part of this title(s), through any social media or file hosting websites.

For all inquiries regarding motion picture, television, online/digital and other media rights, please contact Concord Theatricals Corp.

MUSIC AND THIRD-PARTY MATERIALS USE NOTE

Licensees are solely responsible for obtaining formal written permission from copyright owners to use copyrighted music and/or other copyrighted third-party materials (e.g. artworks, logos) in the performance of this play and are strongly cautioned to do so. If no such permission is obtained by the licensee, then the licensee must use only original music and materials that the licensee owns and controls. Licensees are solely responsible and liable for clearances of all third-party copyrighted materials, including without limitation music, and shall indemnify the copyright owners of the play(s) and their licensing agent, Concord Theatricals Corp., against any costs, expenses, losses and liabilities arising from the use of such copyrighted third-party materials by licensees. For music, please contact the appropriate music licensing authority in your territory for the rights to any incidental music.

IMPORTANT BILLING AND CREDIT REQUIREMENTS

If you have obtained performance rights to this title, please refer to your licensing agreement for important billing and credit requirements.

TABLE OF CONTENTS

About The Blank Theater's Young Playwrights Festival vi

The Legend of Caeneus....................................1
by Zander Pryor

stand. Up. HIT! 43
by Wyn Alyse Thomas

Gray Area 87
by Simone Chaney

Dollface 107
by Jeremino Sutton

Droplets Pellets Bullets................................. 121
by Isabel Beatriz Tongson

Under My Skin..135
by Disha Catt

ABOUT THE BLANK THEATRE'S YOUNG PLAYWRIGHTS FESTIVAL

The Blank Theatre was founded in 1990 by Daniel Henning as a home for writers, dedicated to the production of first-rate theatre, education of current and future artists, and creation of groundbreaking new works for the theatrical repertoire, with a fierce commitment to equality and diversity onstage.

The Blank has been called "one of the best Theatre Companies in America" by the Drama League, was honored by LA City Council for excellence and innovation, and won the Hollywood Arts Council's Award "for pursuing artistic excellence & nurturing the next generation of playwrights."

The Young Playwrights Festival (*YPF*), founded in 1992, continues the mission of The Blank by supporting work by young people aged nine to nineteen. Every year, a Selection Committee made up of entertainment professionals meets to select the twelve best plays out of hundreds of submissions from young people across the United States.

The winning young playwrights receive mentorship from working writers and have their plays fully staged by professional actors and directors over a monthlong festival in Los Angeles each July. Actors who have performed in YPF include Chris Pine, Scott Lowell, Constance Zimmer, David Castañeda, Kat McNamara, Dominic Burgess, Dylan O'Brien, Sarah Michell Gellar, Kirsten Vangsness, Vico Ortiz, and more.

In addition to full productions of the winners, all forty-five to fifty semi-finalists in the program receive full scholarships to the Young Playwrights Academy (YPA), The Blank's online learning program. The YPA experience creates a safe and nurturing atmosphere to empower young people and enrich their writing through hands-on instruction from working playwrights.

YPF playwrights often go on to successful careers in theatre and entertainment – alumni include Tony Award winner Stephen Karam (*The Humans*), TV show creators Kit Steinkellner (*Sorry For Your Loss*) and Austin Winsberg (*Zoey's Extraordinary Playlist*), Grammy Award winning musician Mickey Madden (Maroon 5), and Lauren Yee, one of America's most-produced playwrights for the last three seasons.

YPF has no content guidelines for submissions, giving the young writers free rein to share their interests and concerns, and the Selection Committee's goal is simply to choose the best twelve plays from each year's submissions, leading to festival lineups that are incredibly wild and varied in length, topic, tone, and genre. The six plays collected here from the 30th Annual Young Playwrights Festival are just a sample of the three hundred sixty-nine diverse plays that have been produced over the thirty years of YPF. They can be presented together in any combination as an evening of one-acts, or individually as stand-alone pieces.

For more information on The Blank and the Young Playwrights Festival, please visit theblank.com

A NOTE FROM FOUNDING ARTISTIC DIRECTOR DANIEL HENNING

I founded the Young Playwrights Festival as a space for young writers to express their voices and be heard – to show them that what they have to say matters. We are one of the few national young playwrights programs that professionally produces the work, treating the writers as professionals throughout the process.

I am so proud of the program and the work we have showcased in the first thirty years of YPF, and I am especially proud of all the exceptionally talented young people who were brave enough to write a play and submit it to YPF – whether they won or not.

It has always been my dream to bring this incredible work to a larger audience, and I am so grateful to the folks at Samuel French and Concord Theatricals for making that dream a reality.

~ Daniel Henning
Founding Artistic Director, The Blank Theatre

THE BLANK THEATRE LEADERSHIP

Daniel Henning, *Founding Artistic Director*
Bree Pavey, *Producing Director*
Annie McGrath, *Managing Director*
Paulo Andrés, *Board President*

THE BLANK THEATRE BOARD OF DIRECTORS

Rick Baumgartner
Beth Bigler
Daniel Henning
Pekka Kauranen
Susie Landau Finch
Constance McCord
Angela Oh
Ken Werther

30th ANNUAL YOUNG PLAYWRIGHTS FESTIVAL SELECTION COMMITTEE

Paulo Andrés, Beth Bigler, Karlie Blair, David Castillo, Melissa Coleman-Reed, Major Curda, Aliza Goldstein, Daniel Henning, John Hindman, Cassandra Hsaio, Bjorn Johnson, Michelle Joy Lander, Annie McGrath, Jonathan Messer, Akela Munsey, Bree Pavey, Hannah Prichard, Irene Roseen, Michael Shepperd

The Legend of Caeneus

by Zander Pryor

THE LEGEND OF CAENEUS by Zander Pryor, age eighteen, was originally presented in an online format as part of The Blank Theatre's 30th Annual Young Playwrights Festival in July, 2022. It was mentored by Jonathan Tolins and directed by Melissa Coleman-Reed.

CAENEUS (PRE-TRANSFORMATION) ....Gracie Lacey
CAENEUS (POST-TRANSFORMATION)............ Alex Blue Davis
POSEIDON.................................. Juan Francisco Villa
HIPPEA ....Lizzie Peet

CHARACTERS

CAENEUS – a closeted trans man, child of a king. Clever but lacking the tact and wisdom of his mother. Says his mind, even when he doesn't mean to. He/him.

POSEIDON – the God of the ocean. Really bad at the whole human thing but he sure is trying. He/him.

HIPPEA – the mother of Caeneus. Stronger than she lets on. She/her.

AUTHOR'S NOTES

Although **CAENEUS** is pre-transition in the earlier scenes, for my own comfort as the playwright, he is referred to with he/him pronouns throughout. I'll leave it up to the director whether **CAENEUS** is played by a different actor post-transformation, but **CAENEUS** post-transition must be played by a trans masculine actor.

While I describe the literal location of each scene in my stage directions, the set can be as sparse as you like, as long as there is a communication of water when it's important.

Caeneus' name is notoriously difficult to pronounce. My rule of thumb is essentially pronounce it the way YOU think it's pronounced and you're probably close enough.

The transition of **CAENEUS** can be shown any way you like. Given that it's up to the director's discretion whether **CAENEUS** is played by one person or two, I have left it purposefully vague.

Scene One

(A riverside. **CAENEUS** *sits alone, glaring at the river like it owes him money.* **HIPPEA**, *his mother, enters.)*

HIPPEA. You left this behind.

(She fastens the necklace she's carrying around **CAENEUS**'s *neck.)*

So. What was wrong with this suitor then?

CAENEUS. Nothing.

HIPPEA. If that's true –

CAENEUS. Is it so hard to believe I have aspirations outside of marriage?

HIPPEA. No, but you have no prospects.

CAENEUS. I'm first-born and therefore heir to the throne.

HIPPEA. Women can't be heirs.

CAENEUS. Maybe I'm not a woman.

HIPPEA. Oh daughter, I thought we were past this by now –

CAENEUS. I'm more qualified than any of those suitors who seek my hand. I've lived my whole life on these shores, studied its follies and flourishes under father's reign and you want me to be shipped off with a stranger to an even stranger land?

HIPPEA. I don't seek to rid myself of you.

CAENEUS. Funny way of showing it.

HIPPEA. There is little harder than watching the child you raised leave you behind.

CAENEUS. So I won't!

HIPPEA. You know what's harder though?

Seeing her never reach her true potential. Knowing she has forfeited any chance at happiness.

I'm not your enemy, daughter. But I believe you're wasting away, and every suitor you push away withers you more.

CAENEUS. Ominous way of putting it.

HIPPEA. It's the truth.

Your body cannot handle childbearing past a certain age.

CAENEUS. And?

I would make a terrible mother.

HIPPEA. I – you –

CAENEUS. Why deny it?

We both know it to be true. I'm all sharp edges and anger.

HIPPEA. No one thinks they are cut out for motherhood, at first.

CAENEUS. I think I'm ill-suited to womanhood.

HIPPEA. Daughter –

CAENEUS. Or perhaps personhood.

HIPPEA. Don't say such things.

You could raise heros.

CAENEUS. I don't want to raise a hero, I'd rather be one.

HIPPEA. You are foolish to think –

You are foolish, daughter, but not for the reason you think.

No one should wish to be a hero.

CAENEUS. Why?

HIPPEA. Every hero's story ends tragically. One way or another, they're all struck down in the end.

No hero's story ends happily.

CAENEUS. No story ends happily. There is a tragedy in ending, all endings.

HIPPEA. There is peace in endings.

CAENEUS. Maybe.

I've yet to hear a tale that ends in peace.

HIPPEA. Sometimes I forget what a child you are.

CAENEUS. What is that supposed to mean?

HIPPEA. Simply that you don't desire rest yet.

*(***CAENEUS** *is unsure how to respond.)*

What is your plan then daughter? Do you fancy yourself another Atalanta, outrunning men and love forever?

CAENEUS. I don't wish to doom men over the desire for my company.

But I can and will deny them.

HIPPEA. Not even Atalanta could outrun love in the end.

CAENEUS. Will you force my hand?

HIPPEA. I do not wish to.

But you cannot squander away your entire life hiding from suitors by riversides.

CAENEUS. I can certainly try.

HIPPEA. Please, think on your fate. At least consider it.

I love you. I only want what's best.

CAENEUS. I love you too.

> *(She gets up to leave.)*

HIPPEA. Don't stay out too long.

CAENEUS. I never do.

> *(She exits. **CAENEUS** sits, alone for a moment. He stares at his reflection in the water and in a fit of rage, pulls off the necklace and throws it into the river, alerting **POSEIDON** who enters, unseen by him. He hears a noise, and realizes he might not be alone. He grabs a large stick and brandishes at the noise like a spear. **POSEIDON** appears.)*

LEAVE ME BE.

POSEIDON. I did not mean to intrude upon you –

CAENEUS. What the fuck are you doing in my river?

POSEIDON. *(Faintly amused, playing along.)* I didn't know it was your river?

CAENEUS. I was here first!

POSEIDON. Is that how river ownership works?

CAENEUS. I dunno, ask Poseidon.

POSEIDON. Ask him yourself.

He stands in front of you.

> *(Stunned and a bit scared, **CAENEUS** drops to his knees and drops his "spear.")*

CAENEUS. MY LORD.

Forgive me, I do not know how to address you. My –?

POSEIDON. You could use my name.

CAENEUS. Very well then, Poseidon? *(He winces, feeling wrong addressing a God by name.)*

How may I serve you?

POSEIDON. You are ill-suited to those words.

CAENEUS. Forgive me –

POSEIDON. You need not ask my forgiveness.

It was intended as an observation, not a judgment.

If anything I should apologize to you.

I simply meant you are ill-suited to subjugation.

CAENEUS. Is anyone suited to it?

POSEIDON. On the contrary, some enjoy it.

CAENEUS. But is it truly submission if you submit willingly? I find those who enjoy seek it out, and those born into it find it stifling at best.

POSEIDON. I suppose I don't know. It's not exactly in my area of expertise.

My nature dictates superiority over mortals.

CAENEUS. Yet you are here.

POSEIDON. Yes.

CAENEUS. And you have not yet destroyed me over my insolence.

POSEIDON. Do you wish for me to?

CAENEUS. I am ill-suited to this life, as you say.

POSEIDON. Unfortunately, I cannot accommodate your death wish. That lies in my brother Hades' domain, and I am not accustomed to sharing.

CAENEUS. Why are you here then?

POSEIDON. I –

I'm –

CAENEUS. Go on, I'm waiting.

POSEIDON. You're difficult to talk to.

CAENEUS. So I've been told.

POSEIDON. I suppose I'm lonely.

CAENEUS. How? You're a God.

POSEIDON. God of the sea. Not of love, not of connection.

CAENEUS. My heart bleeds for you.

POSEIDON. You're fortunate I enjoy your company.

CAENEUS. If you're so lonely, can't you just take yourself a wife? Pluck her from the shores, drag her below the icy depths?

POSEIDON. I could.

CAENEUS. But you don't?

POSEIDON. I prefer not to.

That is more my brother's style.

My *other* one.

CAENEUS. Zeus?

POSEIDON. Unwilling mortals rarely survive his bed.

CAENEUS. And?

POSEIDON. And I prefer my lovers to survive.

CAENEUS. You know nothing of love.

POSEIDON. Is that so?

CAENEUS. You –

You're a monster, incapable of love. You can't –

POSEIDON. Is that what you really think of me?

CAENEUS. I am not a fool.

I know the legends. I know the ocean is to be feared.

POSEIDON. Indeed it is.

It is also a thing to be loved.

CAENEUS. As if something all powerful as you would ever need anything.

POSEIDON. I never said need.

If it was something I needed, I could simply drown you and revive you in my domain.

CAENEUS. Do it then.

POSEIDON. I'd rather you come with me willingly.

CAENEUS. How can –

How can you take humans as lovers in one moment and slaughter them in the next?

That's monstrous.

POSEIDON. Perhaps.

Tell me, do you consider the shepherd monstrous for what he does to his sheep?

CAENEUS. That –

That's different.

POSEIDON. I disagree.

A good shepherd loves his sheep. He births them and he kills them, even as he shelters them from storms and wolves.

He is not evil, it is simply his nature.

The sea takes. It also gives.

That is its nature.

(Trying to extend his metaphor to essentially ask **CAENEUS** *out.)*

POSEIDON. And –

And the shepherd loves his sheep. He does not wish to be alone.

CAENEUS. What do you ask of me?

POSEIDON. One night. Grace me with your company one night.

CAENEUS. If I refuse?

POSEIDON. Then you refuse.

I like your...unpredictability I suppose.

I am not used to being denied, but the novelty could be interesting in its own way.

Still, I'd prefer your company.

CAENEUS. May I have some time to think?

POSEIDON. But of course.

Return here tomorrow night, and I shall know that you shall accompany me. If you do not come, then, I shall know you have refused me.

I look forward to your company.

*(***POSEIDON*** vanishes, leaving* **CAENEUS** *very confused and a little afraid. He glances at the river again, then exits.)*

Scene Two

(CAENEUS enters his room. HIPPEA sits, waiting for him.)

HIPPEA. It's past dark.

CAENEUS. I lost track of time.

HIPPEA. It's a river. I highly doubt it was compelling enough to make you forget that night had fallen.

CAENEUS. You'd be surprised.

HIPPEA. What happened?

CAENEUS. Who said anything happened?

HIPPEA. So something DID happen!

What kept you out so long?

CAENEUS. *(Blurting out.)* IMETAGOD

HIPPEA. Sorry, what?

CAENEUS. I met a God. After you left.

HIPPEA. Which one?

CAENEUS. Poseidon.

HIPPEA. What did he ask of you?

CAENEUS. How do you know he asked something of me?

HIPPEA. Gods always want something.

CAENEUS. He wants me. My company, I mean.

For the night.

*(Beat. **HIPPEA** doesn't respond.)*

Well. What do I do?

HIPPEA. Is he –

What does he look like?

CAENEUS. I don't know.

Like a man I suppose?

HIPPEA. Was he handsome?

CAENEUS. WHAT?

HIPPEA. Stop avoiding the question!

CAENEUS. What does that have to do with any of this?

HIPPEA. I was just curious...

What was he like?

CAENEUS. I don't know, godlike?

HIPPEA. You truly know how to paint a picture with your words.

CAENEUS. Why do you care anyways?

HIPPEA. Because this. Is. Perfect!

CAENEUS. WHAT?

HIPPEA. If you win his favor, you could have all you wished for! You could travel to any land the ocean reaches and yet never leave home. You would have power, influence, whatever you wish for.

CAENEUS. Anything?

HIPPEA. Anything.

Gods often reward their favored ones with a wish.

You don't have to waste away daughter. This could be the solution we have been praying for.

CAENEUS. I'm ungainly.

HIPPEA. But not unattractive.

CAENEUS. I can't charm anyone. Even if I wanted to!

HIPPEA. Why did he proposition you then?

> (**CAENEUS** *doesn't have a rote response for that.*)

Come, let's get you ready.

CAENEUS. It's not 'til –

I haven't –

What if I don't want to?

HIPPEA. There isn't a choice here.

CAENEUS. There is always a choice!

HIPPEA. This is the only way everyone gets what they want.

CAENEUS. You have no idea what I want.

HIPPEA. Perhaps I don't know exactly what your foolish heart desires, but I know what's best. For you, for everyone.

CAENEUS. I'm not interested in –

I don't want to do that.

HIPPEA. Most women would agree with you, I find.

But since you're so keen, let's imagine this.

Say you don't go. What happens to you?

CAENEUS. He said he wouldn't –

HIPPEA. Did he swear by the river Styx?

CAENEUS. No.

HIPPEA. Then he isn't bound to anything. Even Gods are bound by oaths sworn on the river Styx.

If they break it, they are at your mercy.

HIPPEA. Without that, they are invulnerable, and oaths are easily broken.

Daughter, do you know what he could do to you if you displease him?

CAENEUS. I don't care.

HIPPEA. What of your people then? What do you imagine would become of them? Perhaps he's fond enough that you would survive his wrath. That hardly guarantees the safety of your people, our kingdom.

CAENEUS. He didn't seem wrathful.

HIPPEA. Tides change. Gods are not to be trusted

CAENEUS. And we still worship them?

HIPPEA. We cannot risk incurring their anger.

CAENEUS. I don't wish to use my body as a pawn in an unending war. It belongs to me.

HIPPEA. It should.

The first time I lay with your father was bloody. I cried afterwards, silently so he would not hurt me again.

I think perhaps violence is the only reason we touch.

CAENEUS. There has to be more to having a body than that.

HIPPEA. Perhaps.

I've yet to find it.

Maybe it will be different for you.

CAENEUS. I don't want to be a mother.

HIPPEA. Neither did I.

CAENEUS. Why didn't you fight him then?

HIPPEA. Who says I didn't?

CAENEUS. Well I exist, don't I?

HIPPEA. I allowed him my body. My spirit and my mind are mine.

The epics talk at length about heroism and perseverance, but I have found that the trait that serves us best is knowing when to yield. Knowing when a battle is worth fighting, and when it isn't.

Yielding rarely features in the legends, but legends are told by the survivors.

CAENEUS. I am sorry.

HIPPEA. Sorry for what?

CAENEUS. For what he did. That I'm a product of that.

HIPPEA. Daughter, I will not tell you what to do. You have asked for my counsel, and I have given you my thoughts. You must decide what you are willing to yield.

(She exits. **CAENEUS** *sits alone and thinks.)*

Scene Three

(The next day, sunset. **POSEIDON** *waits expectantly at the riverside.* **CAENEUS** *enters.)*

POSEIDON. You came.

CAENEUS. Was my company unexpected?

POSEIDON. A bit. But that's what I like about you.

Shall we?

> *(He holds out his hand.* **CAENEUS** *doesn't reach for it, yet.)*

You're trembling.

CAENEUS. I'm sorry –

POSEIDON. Are you afraid?

CAENEUS. I am fine, my lord.

POSEIDON. There's no need for formalities with me. It's only us on this shore.

> *(***CAENEUS*** hesitates, weighing his options.)*

CAENEUS. Will –

Does it hurt?

POSEIDON. It never hurts for me.

I suppose you'll have to tell me.

You know, there is still time. You could turn back.

CAENEUS. I could.

Can –

Can Gods truly grant wishes?

POSEIDON. If you come with me, I promise you'll find out.

>   (**POSEIDON** *offers his hand once more and* **CAENEUS** *takes it. They exit together.)*

Scene Four

(The aftermath of a night spent together. **CAENEUS** *lies in a bed with a distinctly otherworldly feeling to it.* **POSEIDON** *reappears. He's smiling fondly, but also a bit unsure of what to say.)*

POSEIDON. Thank you.

*(**POSEIDON** reaches out to touch him, **CAENEUS** flinches back.)*

CAENEUS. *(More afraid than angry but trying to hide it.)* DON'T TOUCH ME

POSEIDON. What's wrong?

Are you hurt?

(He shakes his head.)

Are you certain?

(He looks beneath the blanket.)

There is – That is. You are bleeding. A bit.

Is the pain really so bad?

CAENEUS. May I leave now? My lord?

POSEIDON. You needn't bother with that, my name is not to be feared, at least on your tongue.

CAENEUS. May I go?

POSEIDON. Not in this state!

I've never –

I don't know how to fix you.

CAENEUS. There's nothing to fix.

POSEIDON. I have done something to upset you.

And I am unsure of what it is.

CAENEUS. Please my –

Ask me anything else.

POSEIDON. How do I make you happy again then?

CAENEUS. I'm never happy.

POSEIDON. Well that's no way to be.

CAENEUS. It's not by choice.

POSEIDON. What do you want?

CAENEUS. I want to be alone.

POSEIDON. In good time. I can't leave you alone in this state.

What if I offered you a gift?

CAENEUS. A gift?

POSEIDON. Perhaps a wish might be more apt. Name it, and it is yours.

CAENEUS. I –

I don't –

POSEIDON. Nonsense. Everyone wishes for something.

For example, I wish to see you smile again.

CAENEUS. You'll give me anything I ask for?

POSEIDON. Within my power.

CAENEUS. You swear?

POSEIDON. I swear.

CAENEUS. Swear on the river Styx.

POSEIDON. That's not necessary. Bound or not, I will grant your heart's desire.

CAENEUS. MAKEMEAMAN

I mean. I want the body of a man. I want to look in the mirror and see the hero I dream of being.

POSEIDON. Oh.

Is that all?

CAENEUS. *(Defensive.)* What? Can't you grant that?

POSEIDON. I can. I just – are you sure you want that, as your wish?

CAENEUS. More than anything. I've never desired anything more.

POSEIDON. You are the oddest human I have ever met.

CAENEUS. Don't mock me.

POSEIDON. I'm not.

It's a –

I like that. About you.

CAENEUS. Oh.

POSEIDON. You are certain of your wish? Once it is done, your family will not recognize you. No one will.

CAENEUS. I want this more than anything.

POSEIDON. Then it is done.

CAENEUS. *(Softening.)* Thank you.

POSEIDON. You asked for something so small. Next time you wish for a fate that will end in tragedy, at least ask for a bit more.

CAENEUS. *(Fierce.)* I will.

POSEIDON. There's that lovely smile again.

Sleep my love, and awaken in the body you've always desired.

*(The lights dim as **CAENEUS** transforms.)*

Scene Five

(A little while later. **CAENEUS** *is packing his things, preparing to set sail.* **POSEIDON** *enters and watches him.)*

CAENEUS. You came back.

POSEIDON. Was my company unexpected?

CAENEUS. Very.

You know, I didn't ask for steel skin.

POSEIDON. You've already discovered it?

CAENEUS. It didn't take too long, once I began training. All the others had at least one scar from an ill fated spar.

POSEIDON. Was my addition unwelcome?

CAENEUS. Of course not. It was simply surprising. I suppose.

You didn't have to do that.

POSEIDON. And yet, I wanted to.

CAENEUS. Why?

POSEIDON. A God must retain some mystery. Even from his favorite hero.

CAENEUS. I'm not a hero yet.

POSEIDON. It's only a matter of time now.

Manhood suits you.

A proper hero's journey, setting sail amongst the Argonauts.

Are you happy?

CAENEUS. It's all I've ever dreamed and more.

Thank you.

POSEIDON. Anything for you.

CAENEUS. Why are you –?

You know, you said only one night –

POSEIDON. And I will not go back on a promise.

Am I not allowed to bid you farewell?

CAENEUS. I am setting sail. On the SEA.

POSEIDON. I have a vast domain.

CAENEUS. My heart bleeds for you.

POSEIDON. Things will not be the same when you return. If you return.

CAENEUS. Is that a threat?

POSEIDON. It is a warning, one you'd do well to listen to.

CAENEUS. You're not a God of prophecy. You can't see the future.

POSEIDON. I still know more than you in matters of fate.

CAENEUS. You can be insufferable sometimes.

POSEIDON. As is the way of the sea.

I want to offer you a way back. That's why I'm here.

CAENEUS. Back to what?

POSEIDON. I only wish to allow you to recant your wish.

CAENEUS. No! It's mine, you swore an oath –

POSEIDON. Not forcibly.

I would never do that to you.

But the path of a hero is an unhappy one. One fated in tragedy.

CAENEUS. So is the path of a woman.

For me, at least.

POSEIDON. Ask me for something else, anything else. I will grant it. Allow me to weave you a story that will end happily.

CAENEUS. No stories end happily. All I wish for is a few moments of happiness before the end. In this body, I can have that.

What is the point in a long life if it is a miserable one?

POSEIDON. Is there nothing I can say to you to convince you otherwise?

CAENEUS. Nothing.

POSEIDON. Nothing I can say to make you stay?

CAENEUS. No.

POSEIDON. Then, please grant me the grace of your lips one last time.

CAENEUS. Why?

POSEIDON. Is it so hard to believe yourself loveable?

CAENEUS. Why must you bring love into it?

POSEIDON. I'm well aware of your feelings towards me.

But just because you felt nothing that night doesn't mean the feeling was mutual.

CAENEUS. You don't know me.

POSEIDON. I know more than you think.

But I am fond of you because I cannot predict you.

I have known humans for a millenia, but I've never known one quite like you.

The sea is a force to be reckoned with.

So are you.

CAENEUS. Thank you?

POSEIDON. You've shown a God very little fear.

You'll be a very brave hero I imagine.

Or a very stupid one.

Talking back to a God is very stupid indeed.

CAENEUS. I know.

POSEIDON. A death wish then?

CAENEUS. I suppose I didn't truly care.

Why did you allow it?

POSEIDON. You make me feel remarkably…human.

CAENEUS. Why would you ever want that?

POSEIDON. Do you really think so little of your life?

CAENEUS. To live is to suffer.

POSEIDON. And to live forever, untouched by anything isn't much different.

CAENEUS. You want pity? The all powerful God wants me to feel sorry for him when there are thousands suffering and dying?

POSEIDON. I did not ask for your pity.

You asked me a question, so I answered.

And the answer is that you make me feel unsure. And a bit scared.

I fear you will reject me, that you will hate me.

And it's been a very long time since I felt afraid.

CAENEUS. I'm always afraid.

POSEIDON. You hide it well.

CAENEUS. I wish I wasn't.

I don't know why you would ever want to feel that way.

POSEIDON. All the best heroes fear something.

CAENEUS. So, what am I afraid of?

POSEIDON. If I guess right, what will you give me?

CAENEUS. That parting kiss you asked of me.

POSEIDON. Very well.

I believe you are afraid to be known. That you have been masked your whole life and you are afraid to let it slip.

That's why you're so desperate to become a hero. Everyone celebrates the deed, not the individual.

*(A beat. Suddenly **CAENEUS** leans forward and kisses **POSEIDON**.)*

CAENEUS. Will I be –

Will I be safe?

POSEIDON. No one is ever safe. But you have the favor of a God, and skin that cannot be pierced. Perhaps it will grant you a bit more time. A few more years of heroism.

CAENEUS. I –

Thank you. I am forever in your debt.

POSEIDON. Don't die until we are reunited, and I'll consider it repaid.

CAENEUS. My lord?

POSEIDON. My love?

CAENEUS. Don't –

Try not to be too lonely. While I'm gone.

POSEIDON. How could I? I am the waves that carry ships from shore to shore.

I will be with you.

Scene Six

(Months later. A secluded river, far from Caeneus' home. He enters, bloody. He discards his armor and begins frantically scrubbing his skin.)

POSEIDON. It won't come off that easy.

CAENEUS. It's been a while.

To what do I owe the pleasure?

POSEIDON. Can a God not visit his favorite hero?

CAENEUS. *(Deadpan.)* You have dozens.

POSEIDON. Hundreds, actually. *(With a wink, jokingly flirting with him.)* But out of all of them, you're my favorite.

*(This makes **CAENEUS** tense up. **POSEIDON** notices, pulling back.)*

POSEIDON. I'm here because you're distressed.

CAENEUS. You don't need to come calling every time I'm upset.

POSEIDON. No I don't. I don't need to do much of anything.

But I enjoy your company.

And I prefer you in good spirits.

CAENEUS. I –

Could you keep someone safe? For me?

POSEIDON. Who?

CAENEUS. There was a woman.

One of the men grabbed her at a port and dragged her back to camp.

I – Well.

Hopefully she's long gone by now. She's in your hands now.

POSEIDON. She'll make it home safely. I'll ensure it.

CAENEUS. *(Surprised.)* Thank you.

POSEIDON. Anything for my favorite hero.

But you were victorious. You should be celebrating.

CAENEUS. I know! I just –

She saw me as a man.

POSEIDON. That did not please you?

CAENEUS. I meant –

She saw me as a threat.

I woke her up and I saw the same pain in her eyes that I –

I –

I like being a man.

I like being allowed anger and sexuality and combat. But,

Being a man shouldn't be only violence.

Women aren't only waifs, men aren't only brutes.

POSEIDON. Perhaps you can begin to change that.

After all, you're a man. And I certainly hope you are not a brute.

CAENEUS. You –

You really see me as a man?

I laid in your bed a woman!

POSEIDON. And I'd happily take you again as a man.

(Trying to hide his exposed vulnerability.)

POSEIDON. Providing you'd be interested.

Of course.

It, it's really such a small thing. To me.

My brother, he readily beds women as an animal.

I fathered a Pegasus!

CAENEUS. I –

You –

What now?

POSEIDON. It's really quite an interesting story! You see –

*(Seeing **CAENEUS** is still upset, and has returned to scrubbing his armor.)*

But perhaps now is not the time for such a tale?

CAENEUS. Perhaps not.

POSEIDON. You've seen battle before.

CAENEUS. Not like this.

It's one thing to shoot arrows into a faceless crowd. Or to defeat a monster.

But it's another when you're attacking a village and a man looks you in the eyes before you –

POSEIDON. You have the blessing of the gods.

CAENEUS. That means nothing.

You murder for entertainment, switching sides between battles because of petty squables, or worse, because you're bored.

POSEIDON. Are humans so different?

CAENEUS. Of course not! But gods should know better! Be better!

Or why should we worship at all?

What makes you better than us?

POSEIDON. We do not ask for your worship.

CAENEUS. That's a lie, and you know it.

POSEIDON. You misunderstand me.

We are not beings to worship for mere existence.

You humans choose to make sacrifices to us and in return, we grant favor.

It's all rather transactional.

We are not – Gods are not a force of good or evil. They simply are, like the waves.

Like humans.

Would you fare so much better? As a God?

CAENEUS. I can't answer that.

You'll smite me for my hubris.

POSEIDON. It certainly cannot be the most blasphemous thing to come out of your mouth.

CAENEUS. I *would* be better because at least I'd try!

POSEIDON. You'd drive yourself mad.

CAENEUS. Gods can't be driven mad.

POSEIDON. You would be surprised.

How would you handle a hundred simultaneous prayers, each contradicting the last? Thousands, millions of curses and praise heaped upon you regardless of your actions?

Gods are not better than humans. They're just more powerful.

CAENEUS. So what's the point then? Kill thousands just because you can, because no one dares stand up to you?

POSEIDON. It wouldn't matter. In the grand scheme of things.

Humans end, it's what you do.

CAENEUS. It matters to them!

It matters to me.

POSEIDON. And yet you take away too.

CAENEUS. I've never seen it up close before.

POSEIDON. You're the closest to Godhood you've ever been, in those moments.

CAENEUS. It's awful.

POSEIDON. I agree.

You don't need to continue down this path.

CAENEUS. I chose it, I'll see it to its end.

POSEIDON. You don't wish to return to your previous life?

CAENEUS. I like sailing.

I like saving people.

I like fighting, most days.

But those people, and they're just people, not monsters, they don't see us as heros.

I don't feel very heroic taking families' food and slaughtering husbands and fathers.

And the underworld they're being sent to is the very same one I am bound for.

POSEIDON. Not necessarily.

CAENEUS. Oh?

POSEIDON. Heroes have a chance at paradise, even Godhood.

CAENEUS. Heroes like Hercules.

Heroes half-God already.

POSEIDON. Not always.

CAENEUS. Almost always.

And I'd rather not be a demigod anyways –

POSEIDON. But you –

CAENEUS. I said I'd be better at it than you! Not that I wanted to be one.

I'd rather a world where we don't need gods I think.

But I'd settle for gods who cared.

(Beat.)

I'm sorry. It's not you, it's just. Well. Everything.

POSEIDON. I do believe that is the first time you have apologized since we first met.

CAENEUS. Oh?

Well glad I can still be novel then.

Don't get used to it.

*(Beat. **CAENEUS** cleans his armor in silence.)*

POSEIDON. I can clean that. For you?

CAENEUS. Oh please I haven't felt this dirty since the night you transformed me –

(He cuts himself off as it hits both of them exactly what he said. A beat, then they both attempt to speak at the same time.)

POSEIDON. *(Overlapping.)* Is that really how you felt?

CAENEUS. *(Overlapping.)* I'm sorry my lord I didn't –

*(**POSEIDON** crosses towards **CAENEUS**, scaring him.)*

CAENEUS. PLEASE DON'T HURT ME

*(**POSEIDON** stops in his tracks. He considers his words.)*

POSEIDON. Caeneus, do you fear me?

CAENEUS. I –

Not as much as I used to.

I fear being in your debt. And being hurt again.

POSEIDON. I hurt you? When? I've never intended –

CAENEUS. My lord. If a master asks a slave to lie with them, can the slave consent?

POSEIDON. I suppose not.

But, you were never my slave –

CAENEUS. It doesn't matter.

My kingdom, my home is not an olden city, nor a large one. It's a speck on the coast that can easily be annihilated by a single storm.

POSEIDON. I would never hurt you –

CAENEUS. It's not about me. I'm the child of a ruler, and that makes me responsible for every person within that domain.

Or it did, anyway.

POSEIDON. Oh.

CAENEUS. It was a long time ago.

POSEIDON. For a God, that was mere seconds.

CAENEUS. Look, it's really not – Yes, you scared me. I didn't know you then and it was almost proof that my life was naught but suffering. That I was a woman to you. To all.

Look if your body was wrong, you wouldn't want to be touched either.

POSEIDON. I suppose not.

CAENEUS. It hurt. Made me feel weak.

But I'm not anymore. I have the life I wished for, and I'm invulnerable.

POSEIDON. But you –

CAENEUS. Just because I made my peace with it doesn't mean that it isn't a painful memory. Or that I enjoy reminders of it.

POSEIDON. I thought what we shared was beautiful.

CAENEUS. I suppose it was. In its own way. The worst night of my life gave way to the dawn of the rest of my life. A much happier one at that.

And...you're the only one who knows me now. Knows my true history, my true past. The rest can never know. Without you, I'd be alone.

If I had a chance to redo it, I'd still say yes. It was worth it, to me.

POSEIDON. You need to return home.

CAENEUS. What?

POSEIDON. The centaurs, they are attacking your homeland. They need your strength and your aide.

That is why I came.

And. I am sorry. For everything.

(He vanishes.)

Scene Seven

(The aftermath of a skirmish with the centaurs. **HIPPEA** *is injured.* **CAENEUS** *enters and instinctively calls to her.)*

CAENEUS. Mo –

My queen! Are you alright?

HIPPEA. Just a bit rattled is all.

It's not the first centaur attack we've had of late, and it certainly won't be the last.

Thankfully, it appears no one was gravely injured this time.

CAENEUS. You're still wounded.

May I?

I know a bit of healing.

(He sits her on a bit of fallen debris and tends to her bleeding head as they speak.)

HIPPEA. You know, you look –

Oh forgive me.

CAENEUS. Nothing to forgive.

How do I look?

HIPPEA. Well it's silly, but you remind me of someone.

CAENEUS. Who?

HIPPEA. My dau –

My child.

Vanished. Years and years ago.

Left hand in hand with Poseidon, never to return.

CAENEUS. I'm so sorry for your loss.

HIPPEA. Oh forgive me dear child, I did not mean to burden you –

CAENEUS. You aren't burdening me.

Perhaps she is not gone.

HIPPEA. How did you know my child was a girl?

CAENEUS. Oh –

I just –

I just assumed.

HIPPEA. You presumed correctly.

CAENEUS. Perhaps she's still with Poseidon. Perhaps he took her as his wife.

(**HIPPEA** *laughs at that.*)

HIPPEA. Perhaps, although I doubt even Poseidon could tame that child.

CAENEUS. Maybe he wouldn't want to.

He's not very tame himself.

HIPPEA. I like to think she's not truly gone. That perhaps she's just a bit...lost.

You know. If she was here. Or even just able to hear me? I'd tell her I love her. That I miss her, and I hope she's happy. That whatever life she is leading I'm proud of, so long as she's content.

Even if it takes her far away from me.

(**CAENEUS** *chokes up a bit at that.*)

CAENEUS. I – uh. I'm sure she knows. Having a mother like you.

I'm sure if she was here, she'd say thank you. And that she loves you too.

(He finishes and gives her a hand up.)

CAENEUS. I hope she returns to you one day.

If she's only lost, I hope you find her one day.

HIPPEA. *(Soft, as he packs up to go.)* Perhaps I've already found her.

CAENEUS. *(Smiling.)* Perhaps.

HIPPEA. Where are you going?

CAENEUS. To finish these centaurs off. They've menaced our kingdom long enough.

I swear to you my queen, no one else has to get hurt.

HIPPEA. But how? All of our bravest men have failed to best them.

CAENEUS. I have the favor of the Gods.

HIPPEA. Very – Very well then.

If, no, when you return, will you call upon me again?

CAENEUS. But of course my queen.

> *(He bows and runs off, as she watches him go.)*

Scene Eight

(A liminal space. **CAENEUS'** *body lies undiscovered, and thus not given proper burial rites and unable to pass on to the Underworld.* **POSEIDON** *appears and regards his spirit.)*

POSEIDON. I take it they haven't found your body yet.

CAENEUS. I imagine I'll be left to wander the earth for quite a while. I don't have any among the living who would perform the burial rites. No one is searching for my body.

The Underworld and I will simply have to wait.

POSEIDON. You'll be happy to know the kingdom is mostly safe once again. You took down many of them on your way out.

You've assured your homeland's victory

CAENEUS. I don't feel very victorious. But I suppose being buried alive will do that to you.

POSEIDON. So they finally found a way to best your skin?

CAENEUS. No one evades death forever, one way or another.

Is that why you're here? To say I told you so?

POSEIDON. No.

Although I did.

CAENEUS. I don't regret it.

It was worth it, even if it was fleeting.

POSEIDON. I believe you. *(A look.)* I do. All of your lives are fleeting to me.

CAENEUS. If you're not here to gloat, why are you here?

POSEIDON. To say my farewells. Why else?

CAENEUS. I'll miss you, when I'm gone.

I'll miss the waves.

You've been the only constant in my life for so long now.

POSEIDON. I –

I didn't think –?

Why are you telling me this?

CAENEUS. Because there is no point in carrying secrets over the river Styx. I'm bound for the Underworld, one way or another, and it won't be long now.

Best to let the past die too.

POSEIDON. You could come with me.

CAENEUS. Not even you can stay your brother's hand.

POSEIDON. He can't enter my domain.

CAENEUS. There are a million other humans. Why continue to concern yourself with me?

POSEIDON. Is it not obvious?

(Baring his heart.) I love you Caeneus.

I want – I have wanted you to return. Since that night.

But I want you to be happy.

I want you to rule at my side, because you wish to, not because you fear my wrath.

CAENEUS. Why would you want to keep me around?

POSEIDON. Perhaps I wish to be better.

Perhaps all gods must be feared, but they can be loved as well. Need love as well. Can be lonely as well.

I'm tired of being lonely.

CAENEUS. And if I say no?

POSEIDON. Then you say no.

I swear on the river Styx, whatever happens I will never hurt you or that which you love.

I have been feared and I never wish to be again.

> (**CAENEUS** *kisses* **POSEIDON.**)

Oh.

CAENEUS. You didn't have to do that.

POSEIDON. But I want to be worthy of your trust.

And thus, the offer stands.

CAENEUS. What would happen to me?

POSEIDON. You'd rule at my side. Together we'd oversee all of the ocean.

CAENEUS. And?

POSEIDON. And. Well. Perhaps we could get a chance to start again if you desire? This time as equals.

CAENEUS. I'll do it.

BUT. I will not play your wife. Or birth children.

POSEIDON. I know.

CAENEUS. I will refuse you, and argue with you. I will speak my mind, even if I don't intend to.

POSEIDON. I count on it.

CAENEUS. I will not be a woman for you.

POSEIDON. I prefer you as yourself.

> (**POSEIDON** *offers* **CAENEUS** *his hand. After a beat,* **CAENEUS** *takes it.*)

End of Play.

stand. Up. HIT!

by Wyn Alyse Thomas

STAND. UP. HIT! by Wyn Alyse Thomas, age eighteen, was originally presented in an online format as part of The Blank Theatre's 30th Annual Young Playwrights Festival in July, 2022. It was mentored by Bob DeRosa and directed by Tor Brown.

LOUISA	Madison McLaughlin
AUDREY	Nikki Castillo
CHARLOTTE	Victoria-Elizabeth
MICHAEL	Ronin Lee
JOHN	Christian Zamudio
PRESTON/AJ	Quentin Thomas
MOM/MS. F.	Jill Remez
DIRECTOR	Jeff Witzke
TIM/THEATRE BOY	Dylan Kodai
ZOEY	Samantha Wynette
HARPER/THEATRE GIRL	Alexa Lomeo

CHARACTERS

LOUISA – Female. High school age or slightly older. A theatre kid and a writer. Loves winning arguments. Cares deeply about others (and what they think of her.) Holds herself to an impossible standard. Small-chested.

AUDREY – Female. High school age. Louisa's close friend. Athlete. Whip-smart. Very knowledgeable on social issues. Wise beyond her years.

MICHAEL – Male. Thirties to forties. Leads self defense class. Very excited. Tries a little too hard to empower the girls, but he means well.

CHARLOTTE – Female. Twelve to fifteen years old, must be noticeably younger than Louisa. Louisa's sister. Laid back. Has a soft side, but doesn't willingly let anyone know that.

JOHN – Male. High school age. Louisa's friend. Very fun to be around, but not the best friend to hold you while you cry or have your back – very much a fair-weather friend. Makes fun of his friends a lot, and it doesn't always come off in a joking way.

PRESTON – Male. High school age. Louisa's ex-boyfriend. Says he respects women so that he can get into relationships (in which he disrespects women).

MOM – Female. Forties. Louisa's mom (and a great one). Was very liberal for the conversative area she grew up in, but her feminist views aren't quite as modern as Louisa's.

DIRECTOR – Male. Tirties to forties. Louisa's theatre director. Doesn't care too much about his students – his show must go on and his reputation must stay intact. Wonders why nobody trusts him.

AJ – Male. High school age. A dick.

TIM – Male. High school age. A dick.

ZOEY – Female. High school sophomore. Confrontational and bold.

HARPER – Female. High school sophomore. A Swiftie. A little reserved.

MS. FRANKLIN – Female. Thirties to forties. Audrey's guidance counselor.

TIME

2019 – 2022.

AUTHOR'S NOTES

Staging

Characters are onstage at all times.

Casting Notes

Casting should be diverse and mindful with regards to race and ethnicity. Louisa and Audrey should play themselves and nobody else. Other actors can play as many characters as necessary, but it is essential that the actors present as the gender listed in their character description.

*(Lights up on **LOUISA**.)*

LOUISA. Hi. I'm Louisa. I'm an eighteen-year-old girl. Woman? I'll go with girl, I haven't paid taxes yet. And I'm going to talk about...that. My life being a girl, I guess. So – well, I feel like I should introduce a little about myself so...um...I was born on a crisp Saturday – I'm kidding. I was born down South, but have lived most of my life in a quite liberal Midwestern suburb. I'm an ENFJ on the Myers-Briggs test if that's something you care about (I do) and I'm a Sagittarius if that's something you care about (I don't – sorry.)

We'll start my freshman year. It was 2019, which I think is important. It had been just long enough since the #MeToo movement that people were aware of and thought about sexual misconduct, but it had been long enough that a lot of people had started to, well, get sick of hearing about it. Those people often thought two things: one, that the #MeToo movement had solved sexism (or worse, that it had been overkill) and two, that men were just constantly having their lives ruined by women crying rape. I don't think those beliefs have really gone away since then, but I need you to know that they were there.

I'm going to trust you all and be really honest with you, because, well, you haven't given me a reason not to trust you...

(She points to one audience member.)

Except for you, sir. I don't trust anyone who can fit their phone in their front pocket. Get it? I don't trust men. I'm really funny, that's another thing you should know. Actually, that isn't even true. The men thing, not the funny thing. I do trust men, just not when they're walking behind me down the street. And I've been told that's not a fair fear to have, because "not all men" or whatever. Although, once my sister said this one thing, we were watching tennis...

CHARLOTTE. The ball boys in women's tennis remind me of a society where men are kept underground and used strictly for breeding purposes.

LOUISA. And I thought that was very funny. So maybe I am part of the problem. It was particularly funny because she doesn't even consider herself a feminist.

(Lights out on CHARLOTTE.)

Another important thing about me. I'm a theatre kid.

(CHARLOTTE calls out from the dark.)

CHARLOTTE. Stop doing your monologue, it's eleven o'clock.

LOUISA. Not sure if it's important to the story, but it's important to me.

(Lights up on JOHN and AUDREY.)

AUDREY. How were your first couple rehearsals?

LOUISA. Pretty good. This is gonna be a good show eventually I think.

AUDREY. I will fight someone for a front row seat.

LOUISA. *(To audience.)* This is my friend, Audrey. She's the strongest person I know. Literally. She's a three-sport varsity athlete. She can deadlift my dad's weight, and he is not a small man. She's kind of a genius. Once she commented on a TikTok about bumblebees and I haven't been okay with capitalism ever since. Plus, she can be funny, too.

AUDREY. *(To audience.)* Why did the horse run to the bathroom instead of walk? Because he had the trots!

LOUISA. Okay, that was a bad example.

AUDREY. Sorry.

LOUISA. And the best part of Audrey is that she is not afraid to call people out on their bullshit.

AUDREY. Anna walks around like some kind of ally, but she doesn't care when her cishet white boyfriend uses slurs!

LOUISA. *(To* **AUDREY.***)* Wait, didn't she post about Black Lives Matter on her Instagram story?

AUDREY. Yeah! It's all performative.

LOUISA. *(To audience.)* So yeah, she talks a lot, in the best way. *(Beat.)* And it terrifies me when she's silent.

(Back in the scene.)

JOHN. Let's go. Unless you wanna skip P.E. so you can do jazz squares?

LOUISA. *(To* **JOHN.***)* John you are literally in the musical.

JOHN. There's a difference between doing theatre and being a theatre kid.

LOUISA. Not to the internet there's not. Just remember that I could destroy your entire social media presence in two seconds.

JOHN. You wouldn't dare, bitch.

LOUISA. *(To audience.)* I love John. He is absolutely one of my best friends, but I don't like when he says "bitch." I think I told him that once, but I don't think I was clear enough. I think he thinks it's okay because he's gay, which maybe it is...but it feels sexist to me. Especially when it's in a "don't be a bitch" context, which it sometimes is. *(To* **JOHN.***)* How would you like all twenty thousand of your TikTok followers to see you as dancing spoon number four in *Beauty and the Beast*?

JOHN. *(Sucking up.)* You're beautiful and sexy, and so, so kind.

LOUISA. Uh huh. Let's go.

AUDREY. Woah, hold on. Asshat twelve o'clock.

> (**LOUISA** *looks ahead of her and sees* **PRESTON** *walking through the hall.*)

LOUISA. *(To audience.)* I guess now's as good a time as any to introduce you to my ex, Preston. He wooed me. *(To* **PRESTON**, *in the past.)* I only want to date feminists.

PRESTON. Well I'm a feminist.

LOUISA. *(To audience.)* At the time, it didn't occur to me that maybe he was saying that only because I only wanted to date a feminist, and he wanted to date me. Now that I say it out loud...yeah, it's a little embarrassing. But like a month into the relationship, he said –

PRESTON. And that's when girls start accusing everyone of rape.

LOUISA. I don't even know what our conversation was about, but then he said that, and I went off. *(To* **PRESTON**.*)* Women don't fucking lie about rape, Preston.

> (**PRESTON** *makes a face.*)

LOUISA. I'm not kidding. One in six women are raped during their lifetime.

PRESTON. One out of six women *say* they're raped. Men are having their lives ruined by girls lying about them, have you ever thought about that?

LOUISA. *(To audience.)* Once I stopped kicking myself for not being able to fix him, I dumped his ass. The day when I crossed him in the hall a week later was early spring of my freshman year as we walked to PE. When we got there, they immediately told all the girls to go upstairs to the wrestling room.

AJ. That's sexist!

(**TIM** *laughs and daps him up.*)

TIM. Ethan said they're doing the rape talk.

AJ. Oooh, they have to tell all the girls to watch out?

TIM. Well, you can't spell harassment without "her ass"!

LOUISA. We went to the wrestling room, and we sat on the floor with all the other girls. Then this man we didn't know talked at us.

MICHAEL. Hello ladies, I hope you are having a spectacular Tuesday. My name is Michael. Ex-Marine. Current father of two beautiful daughters. Current appreciator of the hit show *Diners, Drive Ins, and Dives*. I'm here because your school is offering you an incredible opportunity to learn skills that will keep you safe and help you live up to your best potential. Who run the world? Girls. On April sixteenth and seventeenth, you have the chance to take my self defense course during your normal gym time. You might be thinking that this isn't for you –

LOUISA. *(To audience.)* Fuck yes this was for me. Remember the theatre kid thing? Yeah, well, I was actually into sports in middle school, and half of the reason I quit was that I'm so competitive losing made me want to die. Here's the thing: everyone knows not to fuck with a girl like Audrey, who could send you to another dimension if she hit you with her throwing arm, but I needed a way to show people that I'm not one to be fucked with either. So, you take my competitiveness and desire to prove myself, combine it with my general anger at the patriarchy and that whole Preston thing, and I had a desire to –

> *(Someone holding one of the pads used in self defense courses comes in and* **LOUISA** *kicks it with all of her might.)*

LOUISA. – kick some ass.

MICHAEL. There was an article in the news last week: you can search up "Northwestern Med Student Expelled". He threw his entire career into the gutter all because he was drunk one night.

LOUISA. I can't remember exactly how he put it, but it boiled down to this:

MICHAEL. He went to a party and had way too much to drink and then he took a drunk girl into a bedroom and threw her on the bed, pinned her down and raped her.

LOUISA. The way he emphasized the word "drunk" both times made it seem like he thought it was important for both of them. But maybe for different reasons.

MICHAEL. And then he got kicked out of college and lost a chance at the career he's been working toward for years.

LOUISA. I thought the story was a weird choice to tell a room full of teenage girls. He didn't talk about the girl at all, except to say what happened to the guy. It felt a little to me like he was saying that "getting expelled" was something happening to the guy rather than saying that he was something happening to the girl. I looked over at Audrey.

(**AUDREY** *is watching* **MICHAEL** *intently.*)

We would be talking about this later.

MICHAEL. I don't want any of you to end up like that girl. So take this class, and we'll give you the tools to defend yourself. We'll make you better.

LOUISA. *(To **AUDREY**, whispered.)* Better? Better than who?

MICHAEL. You are strong, and you can become stronger. You can learn to protect yourself. You have power. Don't let anybody take it.

LOUISA. That stood out to me.

MICHAEL. Don't let anyone take your power.

LOUISA. He said

MICHAEL. Don't

LOUISA & MICHAEL. Let

MICHAEL. Anyone take your power. Don't

LOUISA & MICHAEL. Let

MICHAEL. Anyone take your power.

LOUISA. It sounded almost like he was saying

MICHAEL. Don't let yourself get raped.

    (The bell rings.)

LOUISA. We got up and left. Audrey was slow getting her stuff together so we were the last ones leaving.

MICHAEL. So, are you girls going to take self defense?

LOUISA. Definitely.

    *(***AUDREY** *nods.)*

MICHAEL. Excellent. I'll see you next week.

LOUISA. We walked out. *(To* **AUDREY**.*)* Yeah, I had some issues with that. That felt like victim-blaming to me, you know?

    *(***AUDREY** *nods.)*

Are you okay?

AUDREY. *(Soft.)* Yeah.

LOUISA. Are you sure?

AUDREY. If I had just – nevermind. I'm okay.

LOUISA. No you aren't. Did that...*(She realizes.)* Are you – did you – Did he say something that...happened to you?

> (**AUDREY** *looks at her and then nods, tears starting to form.*)

Have you told anybody about it?

> (**AUDREY** *shakes her head.*)

Do you want a hug?

> (**AUDREY** *nods.* **LOUISA** *hugs her.* **AUDREY** *hugs her back, tight.*)

(To audience.) I suggested we go see her guidance counselor, and she agreed. So we walked down the hallway, and I kept looking at her, kept waiting for her to say something, but she didn't. She wasn't crying now, either. She was just staring blankly forward until we got into Ms. Franklin's office.

> (*They arrive in the social worker's office, where they find* **MS. FRANKLIN**.)

MS. FRANKLIN. Audrey? Are you alright?

> (**AUDREY** *dissolves into tears again.*)

(To **LOUISA**.*)* Do you know what's wrong?

LOUISA. I – I think so.

> (**LOUISA** *looks to* **AUDREY** *and then back to* **MS. FRANKLIN**.)

In P.E. they were talking to us about uh...sexual assault.

MS. FRANKLIN. *(To* **AUDREY**.*)* And that triggered some feelings in you?

> (**AUDREY** *nods.*)

Can you tell me what happened?

> (**AUDREY** *clears her throat and speaks quietly, fighting through tears.*)

AUDREY. Um...It was September. At an overnight soccer tournament with my travel team. My coach's daughter, she – she was my roommate and, and we were in our room watching TV and then...

> (*She trails off.*)

MS. FRANKLIN. What happened Audrey?

AUDREY. She climbed onto my bed and – and she stuck her hand down my shorts.

> (**AUDREY** *leans into* **LOUISA**'s *arms.* **LOUISA** *hugs her.*)

LOUISA. I'm – I'm so sorry, Audrey.

AUDREY. I couldn't say anything or I'd get kicked off the team. But she kept trying to get close to me at practices and stuff and I tried to get her away but I couldn't...and then the assistant coach came up to me and warned me against getting into a relationship with a teammate.

MS. FRANKLIN. I see.

LOUISA. So they thought it was consensual?

AUDREY. Yeah.

LOUISA. Oh God.

MS. FRANKLIN. Did she touch you again?

AUDREY. She did one other time.

MS. FRANKLIN. Audrey, I'm so sorry. Do your parents know about this?

AUDREY. No.

MS. FRANKLIN. Do you want me to call your mom?

AUDREY. Yeah.

LOUISA. *(To audience.)* They called her mom, who said she would immediately leave work to come and be with Audrey. Ms. Franklin asked if Audrey wanted some water, which she did, and asked if she wanted to look into pressing charges, which she didn't.

MS. FRANKLIN. Do you need the school to do anything to make sure you feel safe?

AUDREY. She goes to a different school.

LOUISA. I knew the statistics. I would whip the numbers out in arguments like the one I had had with Preston, but, at age fifteen, this was the first time I had a face attached to the number. Her pain was so much more raw than a number. We sat in there for about an hour. Ms. Franklin went in circles with questions that tried not to twist the knife. Finally, Audrey's mom got there and ran in and hugged her.

MS. FRANKLIN. Louisa, you can go back to class now. Thank you.

LOUISA. *(To audience.)* So I left. I had missed all of World History and half of lunch, so I went to find John at the place we always eat. I was still physically shaking as I walked up to him.

JOHN. Where the hell have you been?

LOUISA. *(To **JOHN**.)* I, uh…

JOHN. You made me deliver our Renaissance presentation alone?

LOUISA. I'm sorry, I was at the social worker's.

JOHN. What? Why?

LOUISA. *(To audience.)* I don't like lying. Like, at all. Plus I suck at it. *(To **JOHN**.)* I caught some kids vaping in the bathroom. *(To audience.)* Actually, that was true, for the record. I just hadn't turned them in because I didn't want people to hate me.

JOHN. *(Half-joking.)* You, what, turned them in? You just want to completely rule out the possibility of getting invited to a real party?

LOUISA. *(To JOHN.)* No, uh…Some teachers walked in and saw all of us so I had to tell them I wasn't doing it too.

JOHN. *(Annoyed.)* You couldn't've shot me a text?

LOUISA. *(To audience.)* I just sat there, trying to let him be mad at me. Even if I could tell him, I wouldn't want to. Some part of me knew that he wouldn't be able to say what I needed to hear. Even though I wasn't sure what that was.

(There's a beat of awkward silence.)

*(To **JOHN**.)* My mac and cheese is cold.

JOHN. Ugh, how hard is it for them to keep it warm?

LOUISA. *(To audience.)* I went through the rest of my classes, just kind of quiet. Even though we had a debate about abortion in law class, and I normally would have gotten really into it, I just sat in the back.

(Transition to Louisa's house.)

You know the kind of exhaustion that makes your whole body hurt? That was what I was feeling when I got home and sat on the couch.

*(She sits down. **CHARLOTTE** enters.)*

CHARLOTTE. Did you eat the last of the fruit snacks?

LOUISA. No.

*(**CHARLOTTE** notices something is wrong.)*

CHARLOTTE. Are you okay?

LOUISA. Yeah.

(**CHARLOTTE** *doesn't believe her. She sits next to her.*)

CHARLOTTE. Let's watch *High School Musical*.

LOUISA. (*To audience.*) She knew I didn't want to talk about whatever was going on, so we just sat and watched Zac Efron being Zac Efron, while I sat, not wanting to think or move or anything.* And then I got to that wonderful point where I felt bad for feeling bad. Because I didn't go through what Audrey went through, so I didn't have a right to feel bad. But I did feel bad, because the world is a fucked up place, and I couldn't do anything to stop it, I couldn't even talk about it because it wasn't my story to tell, and I still feel bad about it and I still feel bad about feeling bad, which is why I'm telling you now. Maybe that's a normal feeling. Maybe it's undiagnosed anxiety. Maybe it's Maybelline. Anyway. I'm trying to compensate for my feeling of guilt by throwing humor spaghetti at the wall and hoping it sticks.

(*She takes a deep breath.* **CHARLOTTE** *gets up and leaves.* **MICHAEL**, **AUDREY**, *and additional members of the ensemble enter.*)

MICHAEL. Hello again girls. Who's ready to get this party started? I'm so glad you all decided to come, because we are going to give you the tools you need to ensure that if you're walking home from practice or from a play rehearsal or a party one night and a guy grabs you, you're not going to give in. You're going to make them think twice.

If someone is following you, and you start to feel threatened, yell. Scream. Fight back with your voice

---

* A license to produce *stand. Up. HIT!* does not include a performance license for any third-party or copyrighted recordings or images. Licensees must acquire rights for any copyrighted recordings or images or create their own.

before you resort to using your body. But if nobody is there to help you, or, of course, if nobody cares, it's time to take matters into your own hands.

We're going to start with a simple hammer fist. Can someone come help me demonstrate?

> *(Nobody volunteers for a moment. Then* **LOUISA** *hesitantly raises her hand.)*

Excellent.

> *(He hands her some training pads.)*

(To everyone.) The stance is the first part of your defense. *(To* **LOUISA**.*)* Can I touch you?

> *(She nods.)*

If you're standing like this and I push you –

> *(He pushes her somewhat gently and she stumbles back.)*

That won't do you any good. You will be going down. They will be yelling timber. So you have to start with a firm stance. About shoulder width, one leg back.

> *(He demonstrates,* **LOUISA** *mirrors him.)*

Now –

> *(He pushes her but she doesn't move.)*

Bring your arm up, your fist against your face like this, and then hit as hard as you can, and follow through.

> *(He hits the training pad in slow motion.)*

Now girls, to your feet. Thank you, volunteer.

> *(Everyone stands up.* **LOUISA** *puts down the pads and joins them. They follow Michael's instructions.)*

MICHAEL. Stand firm, but with bend in the knees. Excellent. Arm up – *(To **AUDREY**.)* too much tension, relax a bit. *(To everyone.)* Hit and follow through.

> *(They do, hitting the air. **MICHAEL** grabs the pads.)*

Again. Stand firm. Arm up. Hit. Great, now line up. Everyone gets to hit this pad. I want you to yell at him and yell as you go through the motions. Use your voice and say the phrases we talked about.

> *(They get in line, most excitedly chattering. **LOUISA** moves to the back to be with **AUDREY**. The next line is repeated once for each girl in the line. They follow his instructions as he says to them:)*

Stand. Arm up. Hit!

> *(Each time, **MICHAEL** follows "Stand. Arm up. Hit!" with a different reaction to each girl. Some reaction lines may be cut if you do not have a female actor for each, though option four should be kept in. If you have more actors, the actor playing **MICHAEL** can ad-lib similar responses.)*

(Option 1.)

Don't be afraid to really go for it. Picture whoever you need to picture.

(Option 2.)

Put your back into it. Punch the patriarchy right out of him.

(Option 3.)

I'd be afraid to meet you in a dark alley.

> *(Option 4, taking the girls arm and raising it to the correct position.)*

Right there when you prepare.

> *(**LOUISA** steps up to take her turn.)*

Stand.

> *(**LOUISA** stands firm.)*

LOUISA. Back off!

MICHAEL. Arm up.

LOUISA. *(Putting her arm up, yelling.)* I don't know you!

MICHAEL. Hit!

LOUISA. I said back off!

> *(She hits hard. **MICHAEL** might stumble a little.)*

MICHAEL. Good job.

> *(**LOUISA** smiles, and then moves away to watch **AUDREY**. **AUDREY** walks up slowly.)*

Stand. Up. Hit!

> *(**AUDREY** hits, but clearly without her full force. She does not make any noise as she does so.)*

Use your voice!

AUDREY. *(Not a yell.)* Back off.

MICHAEL. Stand. Up. Hit!

> *(**AUDREY** does, still not full power.)*

AUDREY. *(A little louder.)* I don't know you!

MICHAEL. Again! Stand! Up! Don't let him take your power away! Put your hips into it. Stand! Up!

AUDREY. *(A full yell.)* Get off of me!

> *(In a sudden burst of power, she hits the hardest that anyone has. He stumbles back. He and some of the girls clap.)*

MICHAEL. There it is! I'd hate to be the poor sucker who messed with you.

AUDREY. *(Quiet again.)* Thanks.

> *(The scene ends, **LOUISA** comes downstage. **AUDREY** goes to sit at a lunch table. Everyone else leaves.)*

LOUISA. Me and Audrey didn't talk about it afterwards. Any of it. Every once in a while someone around us would say something about sexual assault and we would sit there in a tense silence, knowing we were both thinking about the same thing but neither of us saying anything. I never wrote about it, except for a really vague diary entry the day it happened. I didn't tell anyone about it. My mom didn't even know for years.

> *(**MOM** enters.)*

It was weird, because I tell my mom pretty much everything. And I really wanted to tell her, to tell someone, but I couldn't let myself.

My mom and I grew up in very different political landscapes, with her in a very very Southern landscape. Plus, she was a pastor, so people assume she's a crazy Christian that thinks women should pump out babies and make casseroles, but actually she hates cooking. And also Galatians 3:28 says "there is neither Jew nor Greek, slave nor free, *male nor female*, for you are all one in Christ Jesus," bitch. People assume that when

I talk about how I disagree politically with my family members that I'm talking about her, but I'm not. We get along.

MOM. I'm with her.

LOUISA. Hell yeah, you are. Our main feminist fights come from clothing. Hold on, I'll show you.

> (**LOUISA** *walks offstage. She pokes her head out.*)

Imagine I'm wearing a V-neck. I'm showing approximately forty-five to forty-seven percent of the cleavage that an A cup can. There's nothing there, but it's low.

> (*She exits completely then walks out.*)

MOM. No.

LOUISA. *(To* **MOM.***)* What? I'm going to a party.

MOM. That shirt is too sexy.

LOUISA. *(To audience.)* When I was younger, she used to spell out the word sexy. *(To* **MOM.***)* No it's not.

MOM. Too much cleavage.

LOUISA. It's not cleavage if you don't have boobs.

MOM. Why are you wearing it? Who's gonna be there?

LOUISA. I'm wearing it because it makes me feel pretty. *(To audience.)* That's usually eighty percent of the reason why. Fine, seventy-five. The rest is that usually there's gonna be a hot guy at the party who I want to think of me as someone other than a girl who plays men in plays and rolls on the ground pretending to be a fucking armadillo in acting class.

MOM. You can wear something else that makes you feel pretty without making *this* the only thing people can see.

LOUISA. I don't feel pretty in my other clothes.

MOM. The patriarchy's winning.

LOUISA. UGH. Feminism is about giving women the choice to wear what they want to wear!

MOM. Well why do you want to wear it?

LOUISA. Because it makes me feel pretty!

MOM. You said that already.

LOUISA. Well you ignored it.

MOM. You're going to put ideas into boys' heads.

LOUISA. Well, didn't Jesus say those boys should pluck out their eyes?

MOM. Well, not everyone lives Christlike, now do they?

LOUISA. What I wear shouldn't affect them.

MOM. But it does. Why would you risk it?

LOUISA. *(To audience.)* It's one of those moments I just wanted to tell her everything about Audrey, to say fuck it I'm wearing what I want, because shit happens to people no matter what they wear all the damn time. *(To* **MOM.***)* So you want me to still dress based on the male gaze, just in a different way. *(Beat.)* Checkmate.

MOM. Haha. Go change.

LOUISA. *(To audience.)* I usually change. Or I just wear a sweatshirt over it before she sees it in the first place.

    *(***MOM** *cuts a look at her.)*

(To **MOM.***)* I don't do that.

    *(***MOM** *raises an eyebrow, then exits.)*

(To audience.) I'll fight her to the end of the earth about why I should be able to be liberated and show my tits. She hates that word. Sorry, Mom. But sometimes

she's right, even when I won't admit it. I do think I should be able to show skin without being scared I'll get raped or making myself a target for blame if I get sexually harassed. I know if she knew about Audrey, she'd understand that that had nothing to do with her clothes. But she's also protecting me. Making sure no one wants to grab me is in the terms and conditions of having a daughter. And she has two of them.

(**CHARLOTTE** *enters.*)

(*To* **CHARLOTTE**.) Do you think Mom and Dad would treat us differently if one of us was a boy?

CHARLOTTE. I don't know.

LOUISA. Easy for you to say, you were allowed to wear leggings way earlier than I was.

CHARLOTTE. Okay, bitter much?

LOUISA. Whatever. (*To audience.*) I'm glad I have a sister and not a brother. Until, like, fifth grade, my mom let me believe that, stereotypically speaking, girls were smarter than boys, because it made me feel like my gender was a benefit to me instead of a burden. But if you have a son and a daughter, you can't exactly just say girls rule boys drool. (*To* **CHARLOTTE**.) What do you think Mom and Dad would've been like if they had had a son instead of one of us?

CHARLOTTE. I mean, they probably would've, I dunno, encouraged him to do different stuff than us.

LOUISA. Like what?

CHARLOTTE. The legos might've gone to him instead of you at Christmas.

LOUISA. (*To audience.*) Side note: although I managed to get by without just receiving "girl" toys for Christmas in my childhood, this year I got an alarm bracelet from my grandparents, pepper spray from my aunt, and, my favorite, a "Fuck the Patriarchy" keychain from the *Red (Taylor's Version.)* collection from my friend Harper. *(To* **CHARLOTTE**.*)* And that would be wrong, right? Because I was a champion at building with legos.

CHARLOTTE. I suppose.

LOUISA. Even though I'm a girl?

CHARLOTTE. *(Sigh.)* Yeah.

LOUISA. So treating someone differently because they're a girl is wrong.

CHARLOTTE. I'm not going to say I'm a feminist, Louisa.

LOUISA. Damn. Thought I had you there.

CHARLOTTE. Nice try.

*(***CHARLOTTE** *leaves.)*

LOUISA. *(To audience.)* Don't worry. She hasn't taken US History yet, so it's just a matter of time. I know that if I told her about Audrey, she'd be supportive. But I couldn't tell her. The only person who knew that I knew was Audrey. The quarter ended, our classes switched, so I saw her less. When I did, our conversations went back to normal: we'd talk about boys or sports or theatre rather than life-altering trauma.

*(***LOUISA**, **AUDREY**, *and* **JOHN** *sit at a lunch table.)*

AUDREY. Louisa, we need to talk about Adam.

LOUISA. What about Adam?

AUDREY. Does he like you or not?

LOUISA. Absolutely not.

AUDREY. Girl, are you forgetting you're a catch?

JOHN. Yeah, no. He's probably gay.

LOUISA. *(Sigh, to audience.)* John says that about every guy that is even a little interested in me.

AUDREY. You say that about every guy that is even a little interested in Louisa.

JOHN. Well that's because it's always true.

LOUISA. John gets a real kick out of my lack of femininity. Everytime the cast list comes out and I'm playing a guy, he loses his mind. It's not just him, though. I joke about it, a lot of my friends do too. I have a couple theories: One, that I'm just not pretty enough to be a girl, a theory which my mom tells me is not true, so ha. Two is based on an observation I had in middle school. Usually the girls that can sing the best get female leads, and the guys that can act the best get the male leads, and I'm an actor first, so that might be why. The casting priorities for girls just feels to me like the theatre equivalent of valuing looks over personality. Like women in real life are just there to please the eyes and women in musicals are just there to please the ears. And I personally am not horribly ugly or a terrible singer, but I'm also not quite a square peg in a square hole.

*(Back to her conversation with **JOHN** and **AUDREY**.)*

JOHN. I'm telling you, he likes men. Actually, come to think of it, that means he might like Louisa after all.

LOUISA. Hardy har.

AUDREY. She doesn't play that many men.

LOUISA. As much as I appreciate your support, take a look at my resume.

JOHN. Zero pussy.

LOUISA. *(To audience.)* My mom hates that word too. Sorry, Mom. Again. I learned the word pussy when I was twelve. From the man that would soon become my president.

CHARLOTTE. *(Enters quickly.)* I would like to add, I was nine, and him and his alleged affair are how I learned what a porn star was.

> *(**CHARLOTTE** exits.)*

LOUISA. Thanks, Charlotte. I was in sixth grade. I and the whole damn country heard him brag about grabbing women by the pussy, and the (not majority but still a lot of) people didn't give a shit and voted for him anyway. My mom said it was because the country hated her *(Clinton)* so much. I didn't get it. If I'm honest, I still don't. Twenty-one women came forward with allegations against him before the election. More have come forward since. That's a lot of fucking people. They said he did it, and he said he did it. And I don't want to bring sexism into this…who am I kidding, I do, but if it had been twenty-one men, I just don't think he would have been elected. I really don't. Maybe it's homophobia, maybe it's because a man's word means a lot more in this world. I think it's both.

That man had a big influence on my life. I had always been a goody two shoes, and he was honestly the first time I realized that just because someone in power doesn't mean they're good. And it doesn't mean they deserve to be. And it doesn't mean I should trust them not to touch me.

If a powerful man grabbed me by the pussy, I think I would

MICHAEL & LOUISA. Hit.

LOUISA. I think so. I don't want to let someone take my power. But sometimes it's hard to know if they're taking it. I mean, my senior year, this year, I didn't know if –

> *(She stops, then looks at the actors standing around her. Everyone except for **LOUISA** exits. She takes a deep breath.)*

My first impression of him was that he let me measure my own inseam. And I thought that was really good because I saw that one episode of *Friends* where they talk about the tailor getting handsy when he's measuring Chandler and Joey's inseams. The first thing that made me uncomfortable was how he talked about my boobs. I was playing a guy, and he asked me what we should do about my boobs. Like if we should bind them or give me a really tight sports bra. Which, I get it, it's a conversation we needed to have, because I was the actor and he was the costume designer. But he wasn't listening when I tried to tell him it wouldn't take much to make "the girls" disappear. He talked about it so loud and for so long, and there was a teenage boy in the room...and I'm trying to keep some street cred, you know? But that wasn't a big deal. But when I went in for other fittings, he would –

(A male actor walks up behind her.)

No. I don't want him in the play.

(The male actor leaves.)

Zoey, Can you show them what he did?

ZOEY. You want me to just...do it?

LOUISA. No, Just like show it, but don't actually touch me.

ZOEY. Got it.

LOUISA. One time he was measuring me for these weird pants, and he just kinda, was like, this –

*(****ZOEY*** holds her hands in fists in front of* ***LOUISA****'s butt.)*

For a long time. Like it felt like it was way longer than it needed to be. But I'm not a costume designer, and it was a weird costume piece, so I still don't know if that was actually wrong at all. But I didn't like it. And then another time, I was trying on a shirt for him. I'm on edge because he had made me uncomfortable before, and he says

LOUISA & MICHAEL. Stand

LOUISA. Over here, and put your arms

LOUISA & MICHAEL. Up

LOUISA. So he could measure, nothing weird happened, I put on the shirt he had from me, and it fit. It was fine. And then he just quickly –

> *(Without touching her,* **ZOEY** *mimes running her hands down her chest.)*

Yeah. So…what was I supposed to do?

MICHAEL. Stand firm, but with bend in the knees. Arm up. Hit and follow through.

LOUISA. He wasn't hurting anyone. They didn't tell me what to do if I wasn't being hurt.

MICHAEL. Don't let him take your power.

LOUISA. What power? I'm not this feminist bad bitch carrying a can of pepper spray down the street. I'm at a theatre rehearsal.

ZOEY. Do you want him to touch you there?

MICHAEL. *(Hammerfist steps.)* Stand. Up. Hit.

LOUISA. *(To* **ZOEY.***)* It's fine, he just doesn't have boundaries.

ZOEY. He doesn't –

MICHAEL. Stand. Up.

LOUISA. There's nothing to stand up for!

ZOEY. But you don't want him to do it, do you?

LOUISA. Of course I don't! But people said he's gay, so it's not like –

MICHAEL. Don't let him

LOUISA. I –

MICHAEL. Stand!

ZOEY. Is he making you uncomfortable?

LOUISA. Of course he is! I don't –

MICHAEL. Up!

LOUISA. – want his hands on my boobs.

MS. FRANKLIN. Did that trigger some feelings in you?

MICHAEL. Don't let him take

LOUISA. He probably just forgot I have boobs! If I wasn't so flat, it might actually –

ZOEY. Stand up!

MICHAEL. Hit!

LOUISA. Stop! He isn't hurting me!

ZOEY. But you said –

MICHAEL. Don't let him!

MOM. Why would you risk it? Get away from him.

AUDREY. I couldn't say anything.

PRESTON. Men are having their lives ruined by girls lying about them, have you ever thought about that?

LOUISA. I'll just let him! I'm not crying "Me Too" and taking some innocent guy's job and making everyone go costumeless just because I'm uncomfortable!

ZOEY. He's doing it to all of us!

(Beat.)

LOUISA. What?

ZOEY. He lifted my shirt without asking. He was screaming at the freshman. He kept making all these comments about how big Tina's boobs are. Everyone's uncomfortable.

LOUISA. I can talk to someone.

ZOEY. I wanted to go talk to the director.

LOUISA. Is he actually going to handle it?

ZOEY. He's in charge.

LOUISA. That doesn't answer my question.

MICHAEL. Stand.

LOUISA. We can go. I'll do the talking.

ZOEY. You don't have to –

LOUISA. Look, I'm a senior, let everyone take the anger out on me if the show falls apart.

ZOEY. They can be angry at me, it's okay.

LOUISA. You've got two more years left. I'll be out of here before no time.

ZOEY. Are you sure?

LOUISA. Yeah. Plus I've been kissing his ass for four years so he'll listen to me. *(To audience.)* I didn't mention that I also wanted to talk to him because I have this self-destructive savior complex, and I tend to think I can fix anything with my words if I try hard enough. As long as I –

MICHAEL. Fight back using your voice. Don't let him take your power.

LOUISA. We'll go to the director. Is there anyone else who you think would want to come with us?

ZOEY. Yeah, I texted Harper, who said she'll come, but I haven't heard anything from –

(**JOHN** *enters.* **ZOEY** *exits.*)

LOUISA. John.

JOHN. Yeah, his hands were on my crotch for a hot second.

LOUISA. Zoey and Harper and I are going to talk to the director about what he did to us.

JOHN. It's not even just you, it's literally everyone.

LOUISA. Exactly! So we were thinking, having you there would make him see it's not just girls. Like he might actually listen.

JOHN. I mean…he was doing my pants so it didn't really bother me.

LOUISA. But like, for me, there was absolutely no reason for him to touch my boobs.

JOHN. What boobs?

*(**LOUISA** doesn't have a response.)*

Sorry. I just mean he was trying to make you look like a guy, so it might have been an accident.

LOUISA. For me, yeah. But one of the girls in the cast had a previous experience with sexual assault so it was really triggering for her. It doesn't matter if it was an accident, he needs to stop. At least for everyone else. *(Beat.)* Just come with us. Please.

(Beat.)

JOHN. No.

LOUISA. John, please –

JOHN. I'm not down to be the one that gets the show ruined.

LOUISA. We're seniors, no one can hate us that much.

JOHN. It's not a big deal.

LOUISA. Are you kidding? This is bigger than you and me.

JOHN. So what, you want us to go and claim that we're these victims that we aren't?

LOUISA. No, I just want to –

JOHN. Use me?

LOUISA. No, of course not.

JOHN. I'm not comfortable talking to the director about my dick when I don't have to.

LOUISA. John –

JOHN. If it happens again, I might. Is that fine, Louisa?

LOUISA. Okay.

> (**JOHN** *exits.* **DIRECTOR**, **ZOEY**, *and* **HARPER** *enter bringing on their own chairs.* **MICHAEL** *brings on a chair for* **LOUISA**.)

So, just Zoey, Harper, and I went. I wished Audrey was there. *(To* **DIRECTOR**.*)* So that's what happened. And I don't want to blow anything out of proportion. I'm not – he didn't –...I want to make that clear.

DIRECTOR. But he did touch your...

> *(He gestures to his chest.)*

LOUISA. Yes. But not like...not in a predatory way. Just in a not-getting-boundaries way. Same when he was touching my butt. It just felt like his hands were there way longer than they needed to be. *(To audience.)* It's not until a moment like this that you realize that you have no idea what to refer to your tits and ass as to your male teacher.

HARPER. And there was the yelling.

ZOEY. And him lifting up my shirt.

LOUISA. *(To* **DIRECTOR**.*)* But it wasn't just us.

ZOEY. Everyone was talking about it. Especially the townspeople ensemble.

HARPER. I heard the leads talking about it too.

DIRECTOR. I see. Thank you for telling me.

LOUISA. *(To* **DIRECTOR**.*)* It wasn't just girls either. It's pretty much the whole cast.

DIRECTOR. Okay, can you tell me who said things about him? We need to know who to address.

LOUISA. Well, it was the majority of the cast.

DIRECTOR. Like who?

LOUISA. Well, a male student was talking to me about how he had been handsy around his crotch.

DIRECTOR. Which student?

LOUISA. *(To audience.)* He actually asked me that. *(To* **DIRECTOR**.*)* I don't feel comfortable saying.

DIRECTOR. If you don't tell me who it is, I can't address it with him.

LOUISA. We asked him to come with us, but he said he didn't want to come.

DIRECTOR. But I can't fix the problem if I don't know what it is.

LOUISA. *(Firm.)* I'm going to respect his privacy.

DIRECTOR. *(After a moment, maybe a little annoyed.)* I need you to at least encourage more people to come forward.

LOUISA. *(To audience.)* That wasn't the last time he said that to me. He told me that more times than he asked if I was okay. And I was okay, but I wish he had shown he cared, because surely he did, but –

DIRECTOR. I can't solve the problem if I don't know what it is. I need people to come talk to me.

(**DIRECTOR** *exits. A beat.*)

ZOEY. Weren't...*we* talking to him?

HARPER. What are we, chopped liver?

(*They laugh a little, hesitantly.*)

LOUISA. He says he doesn't know the problem...but doesn't he?

ZOEY. Yeah, I thought we spelled it out pretty clearly.

LOUISA. I don't know, this can't be true, but it *feels* like he thought the problem was who might say something, not what was being done to the students. He wanted to round everybody up to nip it in the bud before it became a thing. But it was already a thing, and that's what we were trying to tell him.

(**MS. FRANKLIN** *enters. She and* **LOUISA** *sit in chairs across from one another. Everybody else exits.*)

MS. FRANKLIN. So, just sign there to verify that your statement is true.

LOUISA. (*To audience.*) Do you ever have moments where someone asks you if you're being honest and you just think "what if I made up this whole thing? What if I *am* lying and I just forgot?"

(**LOUISA** *signs it.*)

MS. FRANKLIN. I'm sorry we had to take you out of class, the signing is just a formality so we have everything on record.

LOUISA. Yeah.

MS. FRANKLIN. Are you alright? Emotionally, I mean?

LOUISA. I don't want him to get fired.

MS. FRANKLIN. That isn't your responsibility. All you have to be worried about is how you're doing.

LOUISA. But I don't –

MS. FRANKLIN. You did the right thing.

LOUISA. But I don't want us to not have any costumes –

MS. FRANKLIN. Don't blame yourself, you're the victim here.

LOUISA. I'm not a victim! *(Beat. To audience.)* I wasn't. I'm not. He wasn't attracted to me, he wasn't trying to violate me. It wasn't really sexual assault. I didn't go through anything. Not like Audrey, not like other women. Other people.

AUDREY. Louisa.

*(**LOUISA** doesn't hear her.)*

LOUISA. I shouldn't be the one getting coddled and getting justice. I wasn't asking for that. I just wanted someone to listen and make it stop.

I didn't know how much I wished he would be gone until he wasn't. He was still there. He put his hand on my ass again. But the director had said the costume designer wanted to apologize, so don't get it twisted. He definitely had changed.

The costumes took a really long time. Tech week is a time of organized chaos, but people were really wondering if it was actually going to come together at all. Everyone was stressed, including the costume designer. When he saw me in my finished costume for the first time, he cried and hugged me. I let him.

*(She looks at **MICHAEL**, ashamed.)*

I shouldn't have. But I let him hug me. He needed a hug.

LOUISA. I didn't run away. I didn't use my voice. I didn't stand up. I didn't hit. I think I hugged him back, actually. Like a reflex. And then he pulled away, and I walked away. And that was that. I didn't tell the director. I'm not sure if I told anyone at all.

The day after the costumes were finished, he disappeared. Nobody told us if he was fired or not. Nobody even told us we wouldn't have to worry anymore.

(Beat. She takes a deep breath.)

The play wasn't supposed to be about all that. I'm sorry if I spent too much time on it. But I feel like I'm not supposed to be sorry. Sorry. Shit. My whole point was that the people who were made uncomfortable shouldn't have to say things they don't want to. And I'm fucking angry that the director tried to make me cross that line. *(Beat.)* You know what makes me even angrier? That I'm angry at John for not coming forward. Because I shouldn't be. I should respect people's right to tell their own stories.

But you know what I thought when I was telling them about the costume designer? It felt like a dress rehearsal. Like I was practicing for life as a woman. I might have to do this for real. When it hurts a lot more. So I wanted the practice.

I can't know that John hasn't had his own experience, of course. But I just thought, maybe if a guy had been there, the responsibility wouldn't have fallen quite so heavily on me. The director might have believed John if he had said it was the whole cast experiencing it. He didn't believe me. I don't know if it's because I'm a girl. If he thought I was overly sensitive to the issue.

John never learned when to prepare to fight.

MICHAEL. *(Stand in ready position.)* Stand!

LOUISA. When to show you're willing to fight.

MICHAEL. *(Putting arm up.)* Up!

LOUISA. When to do it.

MICHAEL. *(Putting arms down.)* Hit.

LOUSIA. John didn't have to run the show because he's an understudy. Yes, something might happen to him, but he probably won't actually ever have to know his lines. He won't have to memorize the lines we said, the Not to make a big deal but

LOUISA & ZOEY. I wanted to talk to you

LOUISA, ZOEY & HARPER. About him touching me.

LOUISA, ZOEY, HARPER & AUDREY. No, I did not consent.

ALL FEMALE CAST MEMBERS. I just don't want it to happen again.

LOUISA. But just...there are some blurred lines: how do you know when to hit? When is it actually assault? I feel like I could beat the fuck out of a predator... But I don't even think I'd know if a man was a predator. I feel like I'd never know when to hit. I didn't hit the costume designer. I feel like most girls don't hit when they find themselves in an iffy situation.

Do you remember when the ninety-seven percent stat came out? It said that ninety-seven percent of women had experienced sexual harassment or assault. People disputed it, because it was a somewhat small sample, and only surveyed British women, but regardless – what was scary was that I don't know a single girl that heard that number and thought it was ridiculous. I heard it and thought...yeah. I'm a part of that. I'm not saying the costume designer made me a part of it either, because it wasn't sexual or anything.

AUDREY. *(From her chair.)* Louisa.

(**LOUISA** *doesn't hear her.*)

LOUISA. But I've been catcalled. Actually, I am a rare breed – I've been catcalled *only* once. I was fourteen. I hadn't even started high school. I was with my dad, walking through the city. This guy said he'd give me twenty dollars for the night. Which is just so incredibly obscene and offensive and disgusting because…I could make more than that babysitting for two hours. If you wanna prostitute me know my worth, fuck-face.

JOHN. Is that really harassment?

LOUISA. Catcalling was listed on the study as a form of sexual harassment.

MICHAEL. Fight back using your voice.

LOUISA. That's why the number's so high. Because almost every woman and girl has been catcalled.

DIRECTOR. Well then I need you to encourage other girls to come forward.

JOHN. Wasn't it dark out? He couldn't even see you.

LOUISA. I know that, but it counts, it fucking counts! Okay? *(Beat.)* Right? *(To* **MICHAEL.***)* Does it count?

(**MICHAEL** *does not acknowledge her.*)

(To everyone.) Does it?

(Silence.)

Maybe it doesn't.

AUDREY. Louisa.

LOUISA. I'm a girl. I'm going to become a woman. I kind of am already. This country and this world's culture of sexual harassment and assault and shaming of women might affect me one day.

AUDREY. Bullshit, Louisa!

(**LOUISA** *finally hears her.*)

LOUISA. What?

AUDREY. I'm sorry, I know we're supposed to sit here and listen to you tell your story, but you're not even accepting your story.

LOUISA. What are you talking about?

AUDREY. You keep saying that nothing happened to you, that you're unaffected, but clearly you are. I mean, you wrote a fucking play about it.

LOUISA. But it's not the same as – nevermind.

AUDREY. As what happened to me?

LOUISA. Yeah.

AUDREY. Of course it isn't. Sexual assault isn't just the guy at the party pinning the girl to the bed. It's not just guys. It's not just the guys who know they're doing it.

LOUISA. I guess. But I don't feel like I'm this big feminist icon where I can be like, "Look! This is what men have done to women!"

AUDREY. Well maybe #MeToo and feminism and fighting against sexual misconduct isn't about uniting against all the cishet men. Maybe it's just about uniting. Because it happens to a lot of women, so it's a women's issue, and it happens to a lot of trans people so it's a trans issue, and it happens to just a lot of people, so it's everyone's issue. And it's okay for you to claim it as your own.

LOUISA. I can't.

AUDREY. Why not?

LOUISA. If I accept it, I'm putting myself in a category with people who have actually suffered. I just – I feel like a fraud.

AUDREY. Of what? A survivor?

LOUISA. Maybe a survivor. Maybe a woman.

AUDREY. You're not a fraud, Louisa. You are stronger than you know.

LOUISA. Is that a *Winnie the Pooh* quote?

AUDREY. If it is, I butchered it.

(**LOUISA** *laughs a little. Beat.*)

LOUISA. You shouldn't be the one telling me I'm strong. I didn't even know – I didn't support you well enough.

AUDREY. You were there.

LOUISA. But I couldn't –

AUDREY. Fix it? You weren't my therapist. None of it was your fault.

LOUISA. I know that.

AUDREY. Do you?

LOUISA. I'm trying to.

AUDREY. But Louisa, if you think I'm the strong one, why have you been treating me for the last three years like I'm fragile?

LOUISA. What?

AUDREY. You don't come to me anymore. You took so long to even tell me this happened.

LOUISA. I don't know how to tell you I was hurt by this happening when what happened to you was so much worse.

AUDREY. It's not a suffering competition, Louisa. Not with me or with all of womankind, I promise.

LOUISA. I feel like I should claim it. But I can't. I don't know why, but I just can't. Not for now at least.

AUDREY. But maybe one day?

LOUISA. Maybe one day.

AUDREY. Okay. *(Beat.)* Do you want a hug?

LOUISA. Yeah.

>   *(**AUDREY** hugs her.)*

(To audience.) Audrey's story…and my story. They don't fit into the narratives people want to tell about . I'll admit, this would have been an easier play to write if Audrey's story and my story were the kind of stories you'd expect, if some man grabbed us in the middle of the street at night. But self defense and pepper spray and fuck the patriarchy keychains can't prevent all the bullshit in the world. Pain and assault and harassment is raw and messy and shitty and scalding and freezing and lukewarm and ugly and it doesn't fit in a story outline. #MeToo isn't copy and paste. Not every woman or person that's been sexually assaulted has a powerful-man-grabs-woman-by-the-pussy kind of story. Sorry about saying pussy, Mom.

I'm not going to change this play if I have a story like that one day. If someone does something to me that gives me another story to tell. This play is going to stay this little play I wrote at eighteen years old. So you'll never know if I went through something else, because eighteen-year-old me doesn't know what my life is going to look like. I don't know that I'm not going to be sexually assaulted. I don't even want to guess. I don't like being wrong. But I don't want to be right.

>   *(**AJ** and **TIM** enter and set their chairs down in a formation like they are at a table in school. They sit next to each other, across from a chair they bring for **LOUISA**, which she sits in.)*

TIM. *(Joking, making a big deal.)* Rape! Rape!

AJ. Bro shut up!

(He smacks him.)

TIM. I'm being raaaaped.

LOUISA. *(To* **TIM**.*)* It's International Women's Day, how 'bout you save the rape jokes for tomorrow?

AJ. What'd you say?

LOUISA. Just…Don't joke about that stuff.

TIM. We didn't say anything about women.

LOUISA. Well, statistically –

AJ. Great, she brought fucking statistics.

TIM. What, you saying we're gonna rape people 'cause we're men?

AJ. Yeah, not all men.

LOUISA. I know not all men –

AJ. Men can get raped too, you know.

LOUISA. Of course they can. I know that, but you can't just joke about it because women and –

TIM. Damn, I didn't know the feminazis were so sensitive.

AJ. Ha, I did.

(They high five.)

LOUISA. Do you have any idea how many women –

TIM. You know women rape people too.

LOUISA. I know that! *(To audience.)* I fucking know that! I know it's not all men and that women rape and men get raped and harassment goes in every direction but I also know that I have held my keys in my fist when I'm walking at night and I know every single woman has felt uncomfortable because of a man and I know that these boys don't give one fuck about Audrey or people like her! They don't care, because saying women rape people isn't about what that girl did to Audrey. Saying men get raped isn't about what happened to those men. It's about getting me and other girls to shut up. About letting them tell their jokes and pretend there isn't a problem. They don't care about any of it. *(To **AJ** and **TIM**, who, not in character, are watching her.)* So go fuck yourselves! *(To audience.)* But I don't say that. I stay sitting. I look down at the ground. I put in my headphones and listen to some fucking showtunes. I wish I saved the day or cussed them out or did something. I wish I could somehow let them know Audrey is the strongest person I have ever known, but I know that they don't deserve to know her story. I wish I had some great inspiring ending for you.

> *(**AUDREY** enters and puts a hand on her shoulder.)*

I don't.

End of Play

Gray Area

by Simone Chaney

GRAY AREA by Simone Chaney, age seventeen, was originally presented in an online format as part of The Blank Theatre's 30th Annual Young Playwrights Festival in July, 2022. It was mentored by June Carryl and directed by Shelli Boone.

ARIYA	Alana Kay Bright
ESTELLE	Gabrielle Elyse

CHARACTERS

ARIYA
ESTELLE

(Bouncy pop music blares as **ARIYA**, *a fifteen-year-old black girl, scrunches up her wet hair with a towel.* She sways back and forth, mumbling the lyrics under her breath.)*

(She hangs the towel on a hook next to the sink and begins to dance more wildly, with no regard for rhythm or grace.)

(There's an incessant banging on the door. **ARIYA** *doesn't notice, or just doesn't care.)*

ESTELLE. *(Offstage.) Dude,* are you almost *done*? You've been in there like a half hour already. What the hell are you even doing in there?

*(***ARIYA** *continues, dancing her way through squeezing toothpaste on her toothbrush.)*

*(Offstage.) Ar-i-yaaaaa...*Hurry *uuuuup...*

*(***ESTELLE** *rattles the doorknob.)*

(Offstage.) Hey! What does Mom say about locking doors? It's a *safety hazard*... What if a lock broke, trapping my *dear* little sister inside during a *dreadful* house fire? Why, I couldn't bear...the *pain*...the *agony*...

*(***ARIYA** *rolls her eyes.)*

---

* A license to produce *Gray Area* does not include a performance license for any third-party or copyrighted music. Licensees should create an original composition or use music in the public domain. For further information, please see the Music and Third-Party Materials Use Note on page iii.

ARIYA. Just shut up, will you? *(Muttering to herself.)* Such a stupid rule...what do they think we're gonna do in here? Sneak boys in? Make out on the toilet? *(Scoffs.)* And they say romance is dead.

ESTELLE. *(Offstage.) (Pleading.)* Come *on*, Ariya. I need to get in there. I can't be tired tomorrow, but coffee is so *gross*.

ARIYA. *(Over her shoulder.)* Chug some tea, then. You and Mom drink that like you're headed to the chair.

ESTELLE. *(Offstage.) (Pounding on the door.)* Even death row inmates get to shower before they die.

> (**ESTELLE** *pounds on the door again.*)

(Offstage.) Let me *in*. I'm serious.

ARIYA. *(Smirking.)* Oh, wow. You're *serious*.

> (**ARIYA** *finally sticks the toothbrush in her mouth and begins to brush lazily, ignoring her sister completely.*)

ESTELLE. *(Offstage.) (Exhausted.)* Please, Ariya. I'm tired.

> *(Nothing.* **ARIYA** *brushes her teeth.)*

(Rising anger.) Ariya, I swear – Mom doesn't get home until late but –

> (**ARIYA** *sighs and crosses to the door, toothbrush dangling from her mouth, and unlocks it – she doesn't open it. She goes back to the sink.*)

> (**ESTELLE**, *seventeen, enters, crossing to the sink – she is multiple shades lighter than her sister.*)

Was that so hard?

(**ARIYA** *stares blankly at her sister before returning to the sink.*)

(**ESTELLE** *sneaks behind her sister and pokes two fingers into each side of* **ARIYA**'s *neck.*)

Jumper cables.

(**ARIYA** *jumps, her shoulders shooting up to her chin.*)

ARIYA. Holy *shit*...What the hell, Estelle? What are you? In fourth grade?

(**ESTELLE** *rifles through drawers and cabinets as if she'd been doing so the whole time.*)

ESTELLE. *(Shrugs.)* I'd say it's pretty deserved.

(**ARIYA** *stands back, arms crossed, watching her sister with severe distaste.*)

ARIYA. You absolutely murdered the vibe. Like the mood just dropped as soon as you walked in here.

ESTELLE. Good thing it's my turn now. Get *out*.

ARIYA. No way. I'm not done yet. Just wait a minute.

ESTELLE. I don't care. Get. Out.

(**ARIYA** *crosses her arms, staring at her sister haughtily.*)

ARIYA. No.

ESTELLE. Whatever. Move over.

(**ESTELLE** *bumps her sister away from the front of the sink. She turns on the faucet and gathers her hair above her head. She leans forward and wets her hair under the stream of water.*)

ARIYA. Ew. Don't you shower?

ESTELLE. Tonight, no. I'm not stripping in front of my little sister.

ARIYA. You could've been in here before I did. It's not my fault you waited.

ESTELLE. Don't even, you know I've been practicing all night.

> (**ARIYA** *shrugs and takes a swig of mouthwash.* **ESTELLE** *continues to massage the water through her hair.*)
>
> (*Music continues through the silence.*)

What the hell even is this? What kind of bubblegum shit are you listening to?

> (**ESTELLE** *rises, grabs a towel from the rack and begins to dry her hair.*)

ARIYA. (*Mouth full of mouthwash.*) Shut umph. Yours ish worse.

ESTELLE. Come on. Let me play something.

ARIYA. Nompe.

> (**ESTELLE** *rolls her eyes and grabs her sister's phone off the counter. She scrolls through it, looking for a song.*)

ESTELLE. Your playlist sucks, man.

> (**ARIYA** *scrambles to spit her toothpaste in the sink, wiping her mouth and snatching her phone from* **ESTELLE**'s *hands.*)

ARIYA. Sto-*op*. You came in while *I* was in here. You listen to *my* music. All you listen to is rap anyway.

ESTELLE. Call it...*respect*. A celebration of all the work from artists like us.

ARIYA. You always listen to shitty rap –

ESTELLE. Right, 'cause it's not an indie song some white girl made in her bedroom –

ARIYA. My God, just save it for tomorrow.

ESTELLE. Nah, music and art stuff isn't in there. Just your run-of-the-mill, "Equality's great, let's do it!" speech – Principal practically wrote it for me.

ARIYA. It's painful sometimes, Estelle. You just wanna be black so bad.

ESTELLE. You just wanna be white.

*(The two stare at each other for a moment of tense silence. **ESTELLE** breaks it.)*

Whatever…What do you even do in here for so long?

ARIYA. What do you think? Get ready for bed.

ESTELLE. *(Skeptically.)* It takes *this* long?

ARIYA. Shut up.

*(**ARIYA** tilts to one side as she begins to comb her hair with her fingers.)*

Did you see Bella Hadid's new post?

ESTELLE. No, why the hell would I?

ARIYA. True. I should know by now your lack of taste.

ESTELLE. Shut up.

*(**ARIYA** straightens, staring off into space, as if lost in contemplative thought.)*

ARIYA. How can one human being be so *hot*?…Her? At the Met? My *God*…

ESTELLE. Jesus. I swear, if professional fangirling was a thing you'd be a millionaire.

ARIYA. No, I *know*. I'd be so good... Maybe I could *make* it a thing. And then we'd meet – by chance, of course. In a coffee shop or on the street. She'd recognize me for my work, and, of course I'd recognize her. She would realize that no one could ever appreciate her as much as I do...and before you know it my name's Ariya Hadid. It's got a nice ring to it, doesn't it?

ESTELLE. You watch too many K-dramas, man.

ARIYA. And you don't watch enough. Missing out. Romance at its *peak*.

> (**ESTELLE** *rolls her eyes and grabs the towel again to dry her hair some more.*)

ESTELLE. Uh-*huh*. Sounds creepy as hell to me... Can I *please* play something else?

ARIYA. No.

ESTELLE. Please?

ARIYA. No.

ESTELLE. I'll stop making fun of your deformed cat.

ARIYA. She's not deformed... She's just missing a couple toes.

ESTELLE. A couple brain cells, too. I saw her walk head first into a wall the other day. She backed up and ran right into it again.

ARIYA. *(Doing her best not to laugh.)* Sto-*op*. You just said you'd stop being mean to her. That's not funny.

> (*She grabs a product off the counter and squirts a few pumps into her hand before massaging it through her hair.*)

ESTELLE. It's hilarious and you know it. Plus, I'll only stop if you let me play a song.

ARIYA. That's so not true, though. You're gonna keep making fun of her.

ESTELLE. So true, man. So true.

> (**ARIYA** *flicks the side of* **ESTELLE***'s head.*)

(Laughing.) Ow! Dude, that hurts.

ARIYA. Yeah, sure.

> (**ESTELLE** *hangs up the towel and begins to finger-comb her hair.*)

ESTELLE. So how was choir today?

ARIYA. Normal. We sucked. As always. Derek was a jerk per usual.

> (*She bends over, scrunching up her hair in bunches to define the curls.*)

ESTELLE. I'm sorry man…I can't wait for your next concert, though.

ARIYA. *(Rolling her eyes.)* Shut up. That's so embarrassing.

ESTELLE. Why?

ARIYA. How would you feel if you had to get up in front of three hundred people and sing like a bunch of cats going through a woodchipper.

ESTELLE. Jesus, Ariya. That was graphic.

ARIYA. It's true.

> (**ARIYA** *grabs another product and rubs it through her hair.* **ESTELLE** *does the same, after her sister finishes with the bottle.*)

ESTELLE. Well, I'm embarrassed for the assembly tomorrow.

ARIYA. Oh, shut up, you know you're gonna do great.

ESTELLE. Yeah, but I'm the *only* student speaker.

ARIYA. That's impressive, not embarrassing.

ESTELLE. Yeah, right. I look like a suck-up

ARIYA. You are.

ESTELLE. I'm not. The only reason they're having me do it is because I'm the only black kid in the senior class.

ARIYA. You're not even fully black.

ESTELLE. Shut up, I'm as black as you are.

ARIYA. Yeah, sure.

ESTELLE. I *am*.

ARIYA. Genetically, sure.

ESTELLE. Well, yeah. Exactly.

ARIYA. But we're not the same.

> *(Both sisters stop what they're doing for a brief moment, pausing to meet each other's gaze.)*

What? We're not.

> *(She turns to the mirror above the sink, using a finger to part her hair down the middle.)*

ESTELLE. Yeah, but, like, we *kind of* are.

> *(**ARIYA** crosses her arms and turns back to her sister.)*

ARIYA. Anybody ask you to give the pass?

ESTELLE. What?

ARIYA. The pass. To say the N-Word.

ESTELLE. I know what the pass is –

ARIYA. How many times you been asked for it?

ESTELLE. N-None.

ARIYA. Ever been asked if you're part of a gang?

ESTELLE. No.

ARIYA. If you've got any tattoos, *gang* symbols?

ESTELLE. No.

> (**ARIYA** *begins to speak faster,* **ESTELLE***'s barely got time to reply before she's moved onto the next question.*)

ARIYA. Ever been asked if your dad's in jail?

ESTELLE. No.

ARIYA. Teacher's ever look at you during a history lesson? Ask you verify dates on a slave rebellion you've never heard of?

ESTELLE. No.

ARIYA. Your friends ever invite you over because you're the one black friend in the group and doing those BLM photoshoots is "trendy"?

ESTELLE. No.

ARIYA. How many times you been *called* the N-Word? Had it spat in your face with the hard "R?"

ESTELLE. *(Quietly.)* None.

> (**ARIYA** *holds* **ESTELLE***'s gaze for a moment.*)

ARIYA. We're not the same. Never have been, never will be.

> (**ARIYA** *grabs two hair bands from the counter, slipping them around her wrist before beginning to braid one section of her hair.*)

> (**ARIYA** *turns to her sister.*)

Why did you agree to that speech tomorrow?

ESTELLE. Maybe because the principal personally *asked* me to?

ARIYA. Why didn't you say no? Someone else, someone *black*, could've done it.

ESTELLE. I *am* –

ARIYA. I mean, there's not a lot of us at school, but there's enough – we gotta stick together, you know? And enough are upstanding students like yourself that Principal Willis could keep the Straight-A image he wanted.

ESTELLE. I have every right to speak –

ARIYA. You *don't* –

ESTELLE. We may not be the same, but that doesn't mean I'm not *black* –

ARIYA. You just don't know what it's like –

ESTELLE. For *you* – but I know what it's like for everyone like *me* –

ARIYA. Fine. Play like that. Lord knows you're the only one.

ESTELLE. What do you mean?

ARIYA. *(Smirking.)* Whole school thinks it. I mean, you're the headlining act tomorrow, right? Everyone knows.

>   (**ESTELLE** *shrinks, her face falls. Fear seeps into her eyes.*)

ESTELLE. What? Thinks what? Knows what?

ARIYA. Attention, Estelle. You did this for attention. Every black kid in the school is pissed at you, and every racist white thinks you're a laughingstock…Why? 'Cause you're. Not. Black.

ESTELLE. What? What no. That's not – I *am* – not every black is the same –

ARIYA. Nope, that's not all. Honestly, I couldn't care less what they say about you – you chose this. It's about what they said to *me*.

ESTELLE. What?

ARIYA. Derek Henson. Can't stand him. Never could. But after today I've just about had it. "Ariya," he said. Tapped me on the shoulder and I turned around because, of course, he's in the seat behind me. "Where you from?" Huh? "Where you from?" He asked me again. Here, I said. And he said, "Uh-uh. No really. Where're you from?" And at this point I'm already pissed, so I just turn ahead again, but he comes out and says, "It's just 'cause I've been thinking." That's never good. "Your sister. Estelle. She's speaking at the rally tomorrow. The one for Black History Month. Right?" I don't turn around, but I nod. "Right. So what're you? I mean, if she's black, I can barely even *see* you. Like, 'Teacher! What the hell is this in front of me, I can't see a thing.' Am I right?" That wasn't all though. Just wait. "Africa, then," he says, "You've gotta be an African. That's why someone like you isn't speaking. I mean, why worry about…about friggin' *microaggressions* when you've got Apartheid to worry about back home." Try sitting in class after that. An hour's never been longer.

ESTELLE. Ariya, I'm so sorry.

ARIYA. You should be. Not that it does much.

ESTELLE. I had no idea.

ARIYA. Clearly. Still glad you're speaking tomorrow?

ESTELLE. *(Quietly.)* I didn't do this for attention. I promise.

ARIYA. For what, then? Tell me.

ESTELLE. I did it…I did it because…I do. I want to be black. *(She sighs.)* You were right…*(She shrugs.)* I just want to be *something*. I want the world to look at me and be something other than *confused*…I've never been treated like I'm white, but I've never been treated like you, either –

ARIYA. Why would you *want* to? Listen to what I just *said* –

ESTELLE. Just *listen* to me. Please.

(**ARIYA** *sets her jaw but stays quiet.*)

I'm tired of my hair. At sleepovers when everyone's doing each other's, but Lia can't braid mine and my hair's too thick for the cute little updos everyone else does. So I just sit there and smile, pretending I don't see the little twinkle of "I'm sorry" in their eyes. And I'm sick of those stupid freaking checkboxes on college apps – "check your race here" – because no matter what I do I feel like I'm lying. Or –

ARIYA. Jesus. Come off it, Estelle –

ESTELLE. I'm not saying I have it *worse* than you, I –

ARIYA. Not everything is about you, Estelle. You don't have to be the special one all the time. You sure as hell don't want to be special like this.

ESTELLE. At least the world sees you as *something*. You said it yourself. I'm not black, but I'm not white, either. I don't fit anywhere.

ARIYA. I seriously *wish* I had your problem. At least you get to choose. You get to pick what you are, how the world sees you. I've never had that choice.

ESTELLE. But...I don't have *anyone*. I'm not white. Clearly. But...But I don't...I haven't had the "black" experience, either. I don't have anyone to relate to.

ARIYA. Take it as a good thing. The world doesn't know what you are, how to view you. So make it up...Me? They've already got their thoughts about me. But you? You can be whoever the hell you want.

ESTELLE. What...What if I don't know how to do that?

(**ARIYA** *shrugs.*)

(*Beat.*)

I wish I had your hair.

ARIYA. What? Why would you want *that*?

ESTELLE. Your hair looks like it's *meant* to be curly... Mine's just frizzy and weird.

ARIYA. No way, I wish I had *your* hair. The way it falls on your shoulders is so nice. Mine is so big it's embarrassing.

ESTELLE. I like it.

ARIYA. Easy to say when you don't have it.

(**ESTELLE** *shrugs as she continues to braid her hair.*)

ESTELLE. You know who has really good hair?

ARIYA. Who?

ESTELLE. Zendaya.

ARIYA. Ugh, basic.

ESTELLE. No, listen. Her hair – sure, she straightens it and braids it, but when she wears it down, it's just like ours. It's frizzy, but somehow she makes it look good.

ARIYA. Yeah, when she's playing a *drug addict*. The world hates frizz.

(*Beat.*)

ESTELLE. I thought mixed kids were supposed to be hot.

ARIYA. *Right?*

ESTELLE. Like I grew up thinking we'd look like Zendaya.

ARIYA. *Literally.* Why don't we? We're exactly the same.

ESTELLE. *Exactly.* Down to the parents –

ARIYA. White mom, black dad.

(**ESTELLE** *shakes her head.*)

ESTELLE. The universe was on some different shit when they made us.

ARIYA. Seriously, though. I better be so freaking hot in my next life. Like, Bella Hadid hot.

ESTELLE. What is with you and Bella Hadid?

ARIYA. What? She's hot. What's with you and Zendaya?

ESTELLE. *(Shrugs.)* Fair enough.

ARIYA. And I'll be married to Timothée Chalamet.

ESTELLE. Timothée Chalamet will be dead by your next life. Or, like, super freaking old.

ARIYA. *(Shrugs.)* He'll have grandkids.

ESTELLE. *Dude.* You're *sick*. What the hell?

ARIYA. As if you wouldn't do the same thing.

ESTELLE. Fine. Hmmm…in my next life… I want to look like *Lupita*.

ARIYA. Ooh, nice.

ESTELLE. And I'll be married to…Leonardo DiCaprio

ARIYA. Ew. No. *Why*? He's *gross*.

ESTELLE. Not *now* Leonardo DiCaprio. Like *young* Leonardo DiCaprio. *Titanic* era.

ARIYA. Ooh, yeah. *Now* you're talking.

ESTELLE. Right?

(**ESTELLE** *laughs, tying the end of her hair with a ponytail.* **ARIYA** *crosses her arms, staring at her sister.*)

This life or another one, I just want to look in the mirror one day and...and *know* what I see, you know? Like...know who – what I am. Be able to love it, too.

ARIYA. *(Nods.)* Hm. Yeah, me too.

> *(Blackout.)*

Dollface

by Jeremino Sutton

DOLLFACE by Jeremino Sutton, age seventeen, was originally presented in an online format as part of The Blank Theatre's 30th Annual Young Playwrights Festival in July, 2022. It was mentored by Aliza Goldstein and directed by Michael Shepperd.

AMANDA .... Kirsten Vangsness
YASMINE .... Toks Olagundoye

CHARACTERS

AMANDA – a doll that imitates a human woman nearly perfectly, and was raised accordingly.
YASMINE – a somewhat shy, somewhat love-at-first-sight-type woman.
SERAFINA – **YASMINE**, transformed into a doll. Played by the same actress as **YASMINE**.

Int. Subway Train

(**AMANDA** *is fixing her leg, which has been slashed open, by knitting it. There is no blood. She pulls her yarn out of a big tote bag.* **YASMINE** *sits a few seats away from her, but moves closer and sits in the seat next to* **AMANDA**.)

YASMINE. Sorry to interrupt, but what are you doing?

AMANDA. I'm knitting my leg.

YASMINE. Hardly seems like an appropriate place to do that.

AMANDA. Hardly seems like an appropriate place to get your leg slashed open. I was supposed to get off an hour ago.

YASMINE. I'm sorry to hear that. I can pull the emergency brake, if you'd like?

AMANDA. Oh, no, thank you. I don't want to cause a commotion.

YASMINE. But you got your leg slashed open.

AMANDA. But I'm fixing it.

YASMINE. Are you sure you'll be able to get home alright? Your yarn could unravel and get caught on a car tire, or something.

AMANDA. I'll be okay. But if you're concerned and willing to help, can you hold this?

(**AMANDA** *hands* **YASMINE** *a heap of yarn. She looks vaguely uncomfortable for a second,* *but then accepts she'll be holding Amanda's yarn for the time being.)*

AMANDA. My boyfriend is at home, and he is much better at stitching. I prefer his crochet in my joints. It's much easier to walk on.

YASMINE. I think you should be made of knitting. Not crochet.

AMANDA. Why?

YASMINE. Because only you can knit like you. And why would you want another person's identity sewn into your very being? Seems limiting, if you ask me.

AMANDA. But I didn't.

YASMINE. *(Understandingly.)* I know.

(They sit in silence for a few seconds.)

I hope his hands get mangled.

AMANDA. Whose?

YASMINE. Your boyfriend's. I hope he gets in a car crash and braces himself by gripping the steering wheel too hard or by shielding his face and his hands get mangled.

AMANDA. Oh. Well, I don't hope that.

YASMINE. Of course you don't. He's your boyfriend.

(The train stops. There's a voice over the PA announcing the station. It sounds garbled.)

Wait. I think this is my stop.

AMANDA. You should get off, then.

YASMINE. Yeah, I should, but...

*(**YASMINE** looks around, then clutches the yarn closer to her.)*

I don't want to. I want to make sure your leg's all knitted up.

AMANDA. I'm performing self-surgery. Why would you want to see that?

YASMINE. I don't know. I honestly don't know.

(Beat.)

Me and my grandma made a doll once. It was a corn husk doll. I called her Serafina, I think.

AMANDA. Serafina? That's a mouthful. Would you name me Serafina, if I was your doll?

YASMINE. *(Almost incredulously.)* What? You're not my doll. You're a doll who doesn't belong to anybody.

AMANDA. I could belong to my boyfriend. It's like that saying, "What's mine is yours, what's yours is mine."

YASMINE. But I don't think that should extend to your bodies. Should it?

AMANDA. Probably not.

(Beat.)

Have you ever knitted yourself?

YASMINE. No. I'm not made of yarn. I'm made of people stuff. But I broke my arm once and set it myself. Then I went to the hospital and the doctor had to re-break it and reset it.

It was agonizing. You're lucky you don't have bones.

AMANDA. I have bones in me.

YASMINE. Wait, really? Where?

AMANDA. My boyfriend treated me to a porterhouse steak yesterday. I didn't know the bone wasn't supposed to be eaten. So now I have a bone in my stomach.

YASMINE. I didn't even think to think that you had a stomach.

AMANDA. Well, I think I have a stomach. This isn't the first self-surgery I've performed, but I've never had to get my abdomen cut open. So maybe it's just sitting in there? I think it's just sitting in there.

YASMINE. Oh. How…unfortunate…?

AMANDA. Yeah, but I think that's for the better. If I did have organs, the juices from them would seep out through the tiny holes in my knitting. Then I would have to wash my yarn at all hours of the day.

YASMINE. When do you usually wash your yarn?

AMANDA. When do you usually wash your body?

YASMINE. In the shower.

AMANDA. What a coincidence. I wash my yarn in the shower too.

YASMINE. But wouldn't the soap seep deeper than your yarn? If you do have organs, it would go into your stomach and wash the porterhouse steak bone. And not to mention the idea of the taste of your shampoo mingling with the taste of your food.

AMANDA. But what if the taste worked, though? Eating tacos and then washing up with mango-flavored shampoo.

YASMINE. You wouldn't need to wash up for the taste after you eat tacos. Cilantro tastes like soap already.

AMANDA. How do you know what soap tastes like?

YASMINE. My mom had this weird soap that was molded into the shape of a tiny three-tiered cake. It smelled like strawberries. Figured it would taste like strawberries, too. I was wrong. It tasted like cilantro.

AMANDA. I suppose cilantro did come before soap.

YASMINE. What kind of soap does your boyfriend like?

AMANDA. He uses Dove, I think. That or some generic store brand that smells like Dove.

YASMINE. Oh, that reminds me. I read this study once where it was like, men who use Dove were seen as less attractive. But then, women who used Dove were seen as more attractive.

AMANDA. That's weird. Do you use Dove?

YASMINE. No, but I've been meaning to switch soaps for a while. Maybe I could switch to Dove.

(Laughing.)

Hey, maybe I could replace your boyfriend if I used Dove.

AMANDA. Possibly. But I still need him to crochet my leg back to its original form.

YASMINE. *(Almost nervously.)* That-that's all you need your boyfriend for?

AMANDA. No. I need someone to love, too. The superior crochet skills are an added bonus. Can you hold more?

*(**AMANDA** gives **YASMINE** more yarn to hold. She grips it possessively.)*

YASMINE. Well, maybe you could teach me how to knit. I could copy your specific patterns and quirks and hold my knitting needles exactly how you hold your knitting needles. And maybe I could also learn how to love you.

AMANDA. But it's like you said. "Only you can knit like you."

YASMINE. But it's like I said. "You could teach me how to knit."

AMANDA. I thought you only knew how to make corn husk dolls.

YASMINE. I do. I can make a corn husk leg for you, if you want.

AMANDA. No, thank you. Corn husks are weak. I need something strong to help me stand.

YASMINE. I could weave corn husk strips with yarn and make you a leg. It would be stronger, then.

AMANDA. My knitting is stronger on its own.

YASMINE. Then why do you allow your boyfriend to crochet your joints?

AMANDA. He's my boyfriend. And if I told him to stop now, he would think I'm angry with him. I couldn't explain to him that I had an epiphany with a stranger on a subway train while I was performing surgery on myself.

YASMINE. Do you think he wouldn't understand?

AMANDA. No. It's just that not everybody has an epiphany with a stranger on a subway train while performing surgery on themselves. He certainly hasn't. He's human. He has to go to a hospital to get surgery done on him. There aren't any doll hospitals around here.

YASMINE. Huh. That's a weird thing not to have.

AMANDA. Yeah. I was wished into existence, so you wouldn't need a doll hospital for doll mothers in doll labor. Some girl was like, "I want a doll," but then when I came to her door she denied any connection.

I was like, "Why deny your motherhood?" and she was like "I'm five!" It was really bizarre, but I grew up in lots of different foster homes and now I'm here.

YASMINE. Does your boyfriend know this?

AMANDA. No. It's easier to tell a stranger your plights and never see them again than to tell a close and trusted friend and see them every day.

YASMINE. But I...I think I'd want to see you every day.

AMANDA. But you won't. You have a life to go back to. And I do too.

> (**YASMINE** *clutches the yarn closer.*)

YASMINE. At least I can see you in my memory every day. My life and the memory of you can coexist mostly peacefully.

AMANDA. What do you mean, mostly?

YASMINE. The memory of you will be an aftertaste of the real you. You taste like war, and love, and battle strategies, and hidden affairs. The memory of you tastes like an empty barrel of grain, what's left for the mice after a brewer empties the wheat out onto the beer vat. These ideas will taint the other while in each other's presence. I think I like the taste of treachery more than that of an immature, undeveloped, yeasty alcohol.

AMANDA. You call beer "yeasty alcohol"?

YASMINE. Is that really all you gleaned from that?

AMANDA. No. But I think I taste more like an undeserved victory than treachery. Hold on.

> (**AMANDA** *knits a bit around* **YASMINE**'s *leg.* **YASMINE** *ponders this as she runs a hand across what Amanda's knitted. This reminds her of* **SERAFINA.**)

Can't you taste?

YASMINE/SERAFINA. Oh.

> (*Smacks lips.*)

This is true. Sorry for my inaccurate poetry, then. But I do like how you taste.

AMANDA. I'd like to think your memory would taste the same as the real you.

YASMINE/SERAFINA. What do I taste like to you?

> (**AMANDA** *runs her hand over what she's knitted on* **YASMINE/SERAFINA** *and closes her eyes, humming.*)

AMANDA. Two people learning to bake in a kitchen together, but they're both defensive of their eating habits because that's what they grew up doing. But then they slowly learn that if they can curl around each other like quotation marks at night, surely they can hold back their exclamation points in the kitchen. And as they progress in everything, they become a softer font, turning from a rigid Times New Roman to a quiet Lato.

YASMINE/SERAFINA. I like that. I don't want to hear about the taste of my memory after hearing about the taste of the real me. It would be tragic and filled with cracked porcelain.

AMANDA. One of the foster homes I stayed in had a weird lady, and she always told me that fine china is supposed to be seen, but not touched, like how little girls are meant to be seen, but not heard.

YASMINE/SERAFINA. But that weird lady must know that little girls are not made of porcelain. They are much more abrasive and tactile and better at not being broken.

AMANDA. I unravel quite easily, but I suppose that's because I'm not a little girl anymore.

YASMINE/SERAFINA. I unraveled quite easily when I was a little girl, metaphorically speaking. Anything could set me off. I suppose we're opposites. Your yarn could get caught on anything and you could unravel. But human skin is much harder to pierce, let alone unravel.

AMANDA. I suppose. But now look at you. Very yarn-y, if I do say so myself. Which I do.

> (**AMANDA** *runs her hand over the section of* **YASMINE/SERAFINA***'s leg she's knitted over.*)

YASMINE/SERAFINA. Oh, that's weird, isn't it? I'm becoming a doll, just like you. Although, I always thought I would be a corn husk doll, if I were one. Like Serafina.

AMANDA. Maybe that can be your new name. SERAFINA.

SERAFINA. Wait, new name?

> (**SERAFINA** *notices the extent to what* **AMANDA** *has knitted her leg. She starts to struggle, but is trapped.*)

What are you doing to me?!

> (**AMANDA** *starts repeating the same lines for the beginning with the same inflection.*)

AMANDA. My boyfriend is at home, and he is much better at stitching. I prefer his crochet in my joints. It's much easier to walk on.

SERAFINA. What does your boyfriend have to do with this?

AMANDA. Why?

SERAFINA. I – I need to get off, please. Missed my stop. Go away.

AMANDA. But I didn't.

> (**SERAFINA** *stands jarringly, like she's made of jelly. She puts pressure on her yarn-leg and immediately collapses. She starts crawling away very slowly.*)

SERAFINA. Get away from me. What are you saying? Stop the train. Emergency brake.

AMANDA. Whose? Oh. Well, I don't hope that.

SERAFINA. What is this, with your yarn?

AMANDA. You should get off, then.

> (**AMANDA** *slides from her seat and can't use the same leg* **SERAFINA** *can't use.* **SERAFINA** *struggles, but stops as soon as* **AMANDA** *sits on* **SERAFINA***'s legs and starts to knit around her.)*

I'm performing self-surgery. Why would you want to see that?

SERAFINA. *(Hoarse.)* Sorry, please...go away...not me.

AMANDA. Serafina? That's a mouthful. Would you name me Serafina, if I was your doll?

> (**SERAFINA** *tries to curl in on herself, gives a death rattle, and dies.)*

Well. Isn't it fitting that your name is Serafina, now that you're my doll?

Droplets Pellets Bullets

by Isabel Beatriz Tongson

DROPLETS, PELLETS, BULLETS by Isabel Beatriz Tongson, age eighteen, was originally presented in an online format as part of The Blank Theatre's 30th Annual Young Playwrights Festival in July, 2022. It was mentored by Lee Sherman and directed by June Carryl.

SUMA	Davina Colaco
LEE	Gavin Lewis
ALEX	Maddie Nichols
STORYTELLER	Madylin Sweeten
QUESTIONER/OFFICER	Jeff Torres

CHARACTERS

ALEX – age fourteen; any gender; high school freshman, wonder-full, optimistic, stubborn, excited to finally be a high school student

SUMA – age seventeen; female; high school senior, practical, responsible, determined, comes from a loving family and is used to taking care of her siblings, star high school athlete

LEE – age seventeen; male; high school senior, hopeful, curious, uncoordinated, local spelling bee champion, will attend an Ivy League institution for college

STORYTELLER – mid-late thirties; any gender (though should be the same gender as Alex); realist, cynical, in therapy for PTSD

QUESTIONER/POLICE OFFICER – forties; any gender; stoic but gentle, above all sympathetic

SETTING

A magical forest.
A modern school.

AUTHOR'S NOTES

Gender should not be a limitation on casting of any kind. Should the director feel name and/or pronoun changes are necessary, that is, of course, acceptable.

Fantastical Forest – Day Darkened by Clouds

*(The **STORYTELLER** and the **QUESTIONER** dressed in Arthurian-type clothing stand in a fantastical forest. There is a small cave. Trees and brush tightly surround the area.)*

QUESTIONER. Your story begins with once upon a time, correct?

(We hear sharp, pellet like rain.)

STORYTELLER. It was raining. The cover of the trees wasn't enough to shield us from the steely droplets.

*(**ALEX** helps **SUMA** move. Suma wears a semi-red cloak. Having been wounded in the leg, Suma falls to the ground and now crawls.)*

She said:

SUMA. We have to get out of the rain, Alex. You have to. You'll get soaked.

*(**ALEX** assists **SUMA** into the cave.)*

ALEX. Where is everyone?

SUMA. Hiding. We need to hide too.

ALEX. Suma, why are we –

(Something rustles in the brush.)

SUMA. Shhh. You need to be very quiet. Please be quiet. Please.

(**LEE** *stumbles out, carrying a sack of books, and throws himself to the ground. Thunder.*)

SUMA. Lee?

STORYTELLER. It was a knight. He had armor.

LEE. Suma. Oh my god. Oh my god you're –

(**SUMA** *hides her wound underneath her cloak but* **LEE** *pulls it back.*)

I have to tie this off.

ALEX. Here. Use this.

(**ALEX** *begins to take off their belt. Bushes rustle.*)

QUESTIONER. And what of your monster.

(Beat.)

There's always a monster, isn't there?

STORYTELLER. Watch.

SUMA. Where is the monster?

LEE. It's in the fields. I heard it and I bolted for cover.

SUMA. You're not hurt are you? Who else is hurt?

LEE. I'm fine but that monster is devouring everyone. The adults tried to herd the children but it just…It just made it easier, didn't it?

ALEX. What kind of monster is it?

LEE. A shadow-walker. The kind we learned about. First it takes your soul then your body.

(Thunder.)

ALEX. *(To* **LEE**.*)* You're in the rain.

*(**ALEX** pulls **LEE** as much into the cave as he can be. **LEE** examines Suma's cloak. It is redder than before.)*

LEE. Oh god. I have to find someone.

SUMA. No. Stay.

LEE. *(Re: cloak.)* Suma. This is completely red.

(Thunder.)

ALEX. We should go.

SUMA. Hide is what we should do.

LEE. It's coming this way.

STORYTELLER. It was freezing in those woods. I remember. I was shaking. The hair on my arms stood up.

*(**LEE** takes off his bag and pulls out thick books.)*

LEE. They're spell books. You hold them in front and they shield you from the monsters and the rain. It's what I was taught to do. Magic.

(The three hold the textbooks in front of their chests.)

STORYTELLER. Lee was bright. Brilliant. He was a scholar with a bright future. He may have known a lot, but we all learned something that day.

ALEX. *(Reading book cover.)* Beowulf, the epic.

*(Thunder, sharper. **ALEX** covers their ears.)*

SUMA. Lee, take Alex away from here.

ALEX. No, I'm staying with you.

LEE. Quiet.

SUMA. Take. Alex.

LEE. Absolutely not. You will not play the martyr with me.

ALEX. *(To* **SUMA.***)* No! I'll hide. I'll do what you say.

SUMA. I won't make it on foot, but I can stay hidden.

LEE. I can carry you.

ALEX. We both can.

> (**ALEX** *tries to pull up* **SUMA**, *but she winces in pain.)*

SUMA. I need you two to run before that monster gets here.

LEE. You think I can't carry you?

SUMA. That's not what I said Lee! Get out of here!

LEE. And abandon you in a cave to die? Don't even think about it.

SUMA. I'm telling you to. I'm begging you –

LEE. I would never forgive myself.

ALEX. Who will protect you?

SUMA. *(Unconvincingly.)* I can protect myself.

> *(Thunder, louder. Bushes rustle.)*

ALEX. *(Whisper.)* Monster.

LEE. Alex, be quiet. Please be quiet.

STORYTELLER. They said:

LEE.	**SUMA.**
The monster won't get you if you're quiet.	The monster won't get you if you're quiet.

STORYTELLER. So I shut my mouth. I bit my tongue and it bled.

> *(Thunder.* **SUMA** *lets out a yelp in pain.* **LEE** *covers her mouth.)*

LEE. I'm sorry the monster got you.

SUMA. Well he didn't "steal my soul."

LEE. No one takes your soul.

> *(Beat.)*

Who is it?

SUMA. We knew.

LEE. What are you talking about?

STORYTELLER. We read about them. Shadow-walkers hide in plain sight. I should've been more wary.

ALEX. *(Under breath.)* I should've known.

SUMA. *(To **LEE**.)* You were there. He said he hated this place.

LEE. I've said I hate this place.

SUMA. We knew. We should've told someone.

LEE. We couldn't have known he meant this.

STORYTELLER. I remember him. He was never with friends. And quiet.

SUMA. People have to listen to us if we're scared. We could've prevented this. God, he lived among us for so long.

LEE. Him doing this did not once cross my mind.

SUMA. Well that was foolish of you, wasn't it?

STORYTELLER. He was older so it wasn't my business.

LEE. It's not our responsibility to be aware of these things.

SUMA. It's our obligation to protect our people, our friends.

LEE. No it is not! We are the children. We are supposed to be the protected.

ALEX. It's Henry, isn't it?

> *(Beat.)*

LEE. Yes. He is a monster.

> *(The three freeze in the cave. The* **STORYTELLER** *is stuck for a moment.)*

QUESTIONER. And then? The next part?

> *(Beat.)*

Of the story?

STORYTELLER. Guess. It's a story told a hundred times before.

> *(The surrounding trees rustle violently. Thunder.* **LEE** *stands and pulls a branch from a nearby tree. He steps into the rain.)*

ALEX. You'll get hurt Lee.

> *(Thunder.)*

LEE. It's too close.

SUMA. Lee! Don't be heroic.

LEE. I have to protect you both, don't I?

SUMA. You can't save me now.

ALEX. I'll protect her, Lee.

LEE. *(Sad smile.)* Alright, Alex.

> *(***LEE** *readies his branch to strike. Thunder builds up.* **LEE** *exits to fight.)*

(Lightning.)

> *(***SUMA**, *with her cloak fully red, sweeps the cloth around her and* **ALEX**. *Lightning and thunder strike.* **SUMA** *begins to doze off but* **ALEX** *catches her head. Blackout.)*

(Lights up. The forest is now a classroom. The **STORYTELLER** *remains watching.)*

*(***ALEX**, *holding their large book, sits under a desk, shaken. The* **QUESTIONER**, *now a* **POLICE OFFICER** *in uniform, finds* **ALEX** *and helps them out from underneath the desk.)*

POLICE OFFICER. *(Into radio.)* I need medical in the east hall immediately.

(To **ALEX**.*)*

Hello there. What's your name?

*(***ALEX** *does not respond.)*

What's your name? Are you okay?

(The **POLICE OFFICER** *reaches out to* **ALEX** *who hides behind the book.*

Are you hurt?

*(***ALEX** *shakes their head.)*

Do you know what happened here?

ALEX. Rain.

POLICE OFFICER. Rain...It's perfectly sunny. It's...a beautiful day...

(Noticing.)

May I see that? Your book?

*(***ALEX** *shakes their head.)*

I promise you're safe now.

ALEX. *(Under breath.)* If I'm quiet.

(The **POLICE OFFICER** *holds out their hands, and* **ALEX** *reluctantly gives them the large book.)*

POLICE OFFICER. *(Re: book.)* Good lord…Were you studying this? *Beowulf*?

(And then.)

What's your name?

(Into radio.)

I need a counselor over here. I have an adolescent, appears to be thirteen years old.

ALEX. I'm fourteen.

POLICE OFFICER. What?

ALEX. I'm fourteen years old. Where's the monster?

POLICE OFFICER. We got…We got the monster alright?

(Stepping away, into radio.)

Fourteen-year-old stopped a bullet with a book. I need medical and a counsellor.

(And then, gently.)

Can you tell me what happened?

(Beat.)

ALEX. Once upon a time…

POLICE OFFICER. Once upon a time. Yes…Yes, tell me the story. Did you hide somewhere?

ALEX. Under cover.

POLICE OFFICER. Cover? Like a desk? Or a table?

ALEX. A small, dark cave. It was raining. Thunder.

POLICE OFFICER. Thunder.

ALEX. And…Lee walked into the rain. Did you find him? And Suma?

POLICE OFFICER. Suma? Is that your name?

ALEX. No. She was in the cave with me.

POLICE OFFICER. *(Careful.)* Did you protect Suma?

STORYTELLER. I…tried.

POLICE OFFICER. And the rain? Did it sound like pellets? Like on stone or on metal?

ALEX. No. No, it was rain.

STORYTELLER. It was rain.

ALEX. And thunder.

| **STORYTELLER.** | **ALEX.** |
| But it was rain. | But it was rain. |

Under My Skin

by Disha Catt

UNDER MY SKIN by Disha Catt, age sixteen, was originally presented in an online format as part of The Blank Theatre's 30th Annual Young Playwrights Festival in July, 2022. It was mentored by Tessa Williams and directed by Jillian Terwedo-Malsbury.

DRAUPADI . . . . Sharmita Bhattacharya
ALICE. . . . . Cait Pool
SANVI . . . . Gita Reddy
MARIE . . . . Marguerite Moreau
HOLLY . . . . Vico Ortiz
PREGNANT WOMAN . . . . Piper Gillen

CHARACTERS

- **MARIE (ALICE'S MOM)** – She is wearing a long black coat. Her fashion is very conservative, and yet, she maintains an air of poshness around her. She has blond hair tied back into a slick ponytail and she has a beige scarf around her neck. She is wearing a cross around her neck. She is carrying a black tote bag and wears brown boots.
- **ALICE** – She is wearing a baby blue slip dress with a white cardigan that hangs loosely on her elbows. She has pearl earrings in her ear, and upon further inspection, you can find a tattoo of a rabbit's ears behind hers. She wears a black, spiked watch. She has white chunky Maryjane's, and you can see a sneak of ripped fishnet stockings on her legs. Her hair is in a half up-do, with half her hair in a bun and the other half messily hanging. She is female, sixteen to seventeen years of age, white, and short.
- **DRAUPADI** – She is wearing black yoga-leggings and dainty studs. She has on a long graphic t-shirt and her black hair is long and left on her shoulders. She is wearing green air-forces. She is female, sixteen to seventeen years of age, Indian, and tall. She is incredibly curvy.
- **SANVI (DRAUPADI'S MOM)** – She is wearing jeans and a black zip-sweater. Underneath her sweater, she is wearing a floral blouse. She is Indian, in her late forties, and short. She has her hair tied into a ponytail at her back, and she has multiple ear piercings, including a nose piercing. She has a pair of black running shoes on.
- **HOLLY** – She is the complete opposite of someone who would own a bra shop. She has hiking shoes on, cargo shorts, a loose-purple exercise shirt, with a green puffer vest, and circular glasses that are held together by a beaded eyeglass retainer. Her white hair is in a pixie cut.
- **PREGNANT WOMAN** – She is wearing simple dress pants and a fashionable maternity top. She is visibly pregnant. Her ethnicity is ambiguous.
- **MEN** – There are two of them. They are tall, older, any age. They are clearly white. They are wearing black suits and ties, with rectangular framed sunglasses.

*(AT RISE: The stage is dimly lit. Downstage Right there is a spotlight on an outdoor-chalkboard-folded sign with the name, "Under my Skin," in swooping cursive letters, with "by Holly" in smaller block letters underneath it. It's a bra shop, with all sorts of lingerie and bare necessities required to make any person who wears a bra, feel comfortable. There is a small potted plant next to the sign, as well as other porch decorations that make the outside of the shop seem very aesthetic. The rest of the stage is dark. Enter **ALICE** and **MARIE** into the spotlight.)*

MARIE. Your cardigan is slipping, dear.

ALICE. Sorry mother.

MARIE. Let me fix it for you. You don't want to be seen looking homeless.

*(**MARIE** motions to touch **ALICE** on her arms to pull up her cardigan, but **ALICE** visibly flinches and recoils.)*

ALICE. I can take care of it Mother. See?

*(**ALICE** pulls up her cardigan and wraps it around herself with her arms.)*

All snuggly and secure. Just like Jesus when he was nailed to a cross.

MARIE. Don't say such stuff like that. Especially about the Lord. It's incredibly disrespectful.

ALICE. More disrespectful than porn?

MARIE. I swear to God Alice. If you don't behave today, I won't let your ass out of the house for a week.

ALICE. Alright mother. If you say so.

MARIE. I do say so. Shall we stop loitering and go inside now?

ALICE. If you say so.

> (**MARIE** *walks out of the spotlight, and the opening of a door is heard.* **ALICE** *stares after her in longing. She rolls up the sleeves of her cardigan and hikes up the bottom of her dress. Just enough that it's noticeable.*)

(With a long sigh.) You do say so. You always say so.

MARIE. *(Offstage.)* Alice! Stop standing out there and come inside.

ALICE. *(To the audience.)* And I always follow. The job of my empty being is to tread behind my mother, forever behind. Forever following.

I'm coming Mother. I'm right behind you.

> (**ALICE** *walks out of the spotlight. Enter* **SANVI**, *dragging* **DRAUPADI** *into the spotlight by her arm.*)

DRAUPADI. Let me go Ma! You should probably know this, but dragging me around is a violation of my human rights!

SANVI. Stop being so dramatic *kanna*. Between you and your father, I have to deal with an entire production of exaggerations.

DRAUPADI. *(Throwing a silent fit.) Amma*!

SANVI. Calm down Draupadi. You need new bras. We are here for new bras.

DRAUPADI. The bras I have are…fine. Completely fine.

SANVI. You complain about your back all the time. You can't exercise, you can't fit into anything, you can't –

DRAUPADI. Jesus, you don't need to spell out all of my problems for me.

SANVI. Not Jesus. *Vishnu.*

DRAUPADI. It's just some good-natured, American slang, *Amma*. I'm not turning Christian on you.

SANVI. If you did, God knows your *Amamma* would have a heart attack.

DRAUPADI. *(Edging away from the spotlight, slowly.)* Be happy that I just saved her then. You know, I just miss her so much right now, that I think I'm going to hop on a plane to India right now –

SANVI. *Kanna.* Be serious, alright? You always complain about the pain. How are you going to wear nice dresses if you don't have a proper bra?

DRAUPADI. I know Ma, I know. I just – I can't help but being a little scared. What if…just, what if?

SANVI. What if *what*?

DRAUPADI. I don't know what…well, I do know, but, what if I can't find anything? What if I don't have a size?

(The light slightly shifts, becoming dreamy.)

(To the audience.) Everywhere else I've been to, nothing fits. My back still hurts. I'm unable to run. I can't wear all the nice dresses the other girls wear, and I can't help but feeling so left out. *(To* **SANVI.***)* I feel like an anomaly –

SANVI. You're not an anomaly Draupadi. You are anything but. You are a light, you are the shadow that it casts, you are your namesake. If we can't find anything here, then I promise, I'll scour the earth just for you.

DRAUPADI. Now whose being dramatic?

(They both pause, looking at each other. After a few seconds, they erupt into giggles.)

SANVI. Are we ready to go in now?

*(**DRAUPADI** looks at her hands, and she takes **SANVI**'s hand in hers, leading her out of the spotlight. The spotlight fades and the stage lights, revealing the sunny interior of the bra shop. There are racks upon racks upon racks of bras, underwear, and other lingerie. All around the store, there are mannequins donning comfortable two-piece lingerie sets. There are dressing curtains on one corner of the store. In the other corner, there is a cash register onto of a long table with many stacks of bras on it. In front of it, there is a red couch with a side table covered in lingerie magazines. **MARIE** is riffling through some bras next to **ALICE**, who sits stiffly on the couch and looks straight down at her hands. **HOLLY** is by some of the bra racks pulling out multiple maternity bras and handing them to the **PREGNANT WOMAN**.)*

HOLLY. *(To **MARIE**.)* Anyways, it's no big deal. Maybe I just have that kind of face. You know, you totally look like a Jane. Or even a Stella.

MARIE. I still feel terrible. How could I be that ignorant?

HOLLY. It's just a name, honey. There are for more important things out in the world. But you know, maybe I do look like a Leslie. I swear to Venus that you are not the only person who has come into my shop thinking that my name is Leslie. Maybe it's the hair, but ugh, it can't even be that. I have a girlfriend whose middle name is Leslie, and her hair is all silky and wavy, so it's definitely not that.

Hello! How can I help you?

SANVI. Hi, we are here to buy some bras for my daughter, Draupadi.

> (**SANVI** *pushes* **DRAUPADI** *in front of her.* **DRAUPADI** *looks embarrassed.*)

HOLLY. Great! You're not the only mother-daughter team that's in today. Have a seat and I'll get started with y'all after I help these ladies here.

SANVI. Thank you!

> (**SANVI** *and* **DRAUPADI** *sit on the couch, sitting away from* **ALICE**.)

HOLLY. *(To the* **PREGNANT WOMAN**.*)* Anyways, we have a new selection of maternity bras, and they are so comfy! I had a girl in here the other day, and she just loved these soft pink balconette bras we had. So cute –

ALICE. *(Scoffs.)* Cute?

MARIE. Alice, we can't go around interrupting people like that.

ALICE. Sorry mother.

HOLLY. No, it's quite alright Marie.

> (**HOLLY** *rummages through the racks to find a couple bras and hands them to* **PREGNANT WOMAN**.)

PREGNANT WOMAN. Thank you so much Leslie.

> (**ALICE** *starts to snicker, while* **MARIE** *gives her a disapproving look.*)

HOLLY. *(Mutters exasperatedly)* It's Holly!

> (*The lights dim and the characters freeze, with* **HOLLY** *being put under a spotlight.*)

HOLLY. *(To the audience.)* Maybe it's the fact that Leslie is such an old-fashioned name or, well, have my wrinkles covered up my identity? Am I old? Has my name succumbed to invisibility; is my body, my being, indifferent?

> *(The lighting returns to normal and* **HOLLY** *looks from the racks to find that* **DRAUPADI** *and* **SANVI** *have entered the shop.)*

PREGNANT WOMAN. Ever since I started my first trimester, my boobs have felt so huge. My straps were digging into my rib cage and everything.

HOLLY. I know honey. You had boob-spillage. Lots of girls have all sorts of bra fitting problems they never get fixed. It's also super important that you have a comfortable pregnancy. Besides, boobs grow. It's normal.

ALICE. How much did yours grow?

PREGNANT WOMAN. Mine?

ALICE. Do you see anyone else in here that's pregnant?

MARIE. *(To* **PREGNANT WOMAN.***)* I'm so sorry about my daughter. She has terribly bad manners. So embarrassing. It causes everyone so much trouble!

PREGNANT WOMAN. *(Hesitantly.)* It's alright. They grew…a couple cups…I think?

> *(***ALICE** *clutches her stomach rather animatedly.)*

ALICE. I think I'm going to be sick.

DRAUPADI. They're just Boobs. They grow. It's not something to be ashamed of.

MARIE. *(To* **ALICE.***)* Alice. You mustn't be rude in public. *(Only for* **ALICE** *to hear.)* Pull yourself together!

ALICE. I just can't fucking be in here right now.

(**ALICE** *runs out of the store and goes offstage. There is a pause of silence.*)

MARIE. I'm so sorry. We've tried to correct her embarrassing temper tantrums at home, but she's just in her rebellious teenage stage right now. It's very inconvenient.

PREGNANT WOMAN. *(Rubbing her stomach, slightly disturbed.)* It's fine. I was worse as a teen. I think it's going to be even more fun to see what this one's like.

HOLLY. Just give her a second to calm down. I'm sure she'll be perfectly fine real soon.

MARIE. She's not your daughter.

HOLLY. Right. You are right. Well, I can help you check out, and Marie, why don't you sit down for a second. Our other mother-daughter team can go get situated in one of our dressing rooms.

(**MARIE** *sits down, and fidgets for a few seconds. However, she stands up and goes outside the shop.* **DRAUPADI** *steps into a fitting room, while* **SANVI** *waits outside. After the* **PREGNANT WOMAN** *leaves,* **HOLLY** *walks into the fitting room. The audience can see the ladies inside the fitting room.*)

I just want to let you know that this is a safe space, but in order to find a proper bra, you'll need to be a little vulnerable here. Are you okay with that?

DRAUPADI. You need me to take off my shirt, don't you?

HOLLY. *(Laughs.)* Yes.

(**DRAUPADI** *takes off her shirt.*)

Have you ever done a bra fitting before?

DRAUPADI. Victoria's Secret a couple times over the years. The last time I went was like...a year ago? They said

I was a 30E, but they obviously didn't have that size. This one's a 30E I bought online a year ago, but it really hurts to wear.

HOLLY. That's not surprising. The bra measurements they take there are not accurate. There's a whole art to bra fitting that people don't quite understand, and places like that aren't inclusive.

DRAUPADI. *(In awe.)* Really?

HOLLY. Well just looking at you, I bet we could try a 28G. You seem like you have a ton of bra-spillage, and your band is too loose, which is probably why your back hurts a ton. You don't have enough support. It happens when your straps are carrying the weight of your entire chest.

DRAUPADI. 28G? But that's, I mean, that's really disproportionate. I don't think I've ever heard of a size like that. That can't be real.

HOLLY. But it totally is honey. I've actually had so many girls come in with sizes like that. It just means your rib cage is smaller than your bust. It's a lot more normal than you think. Even I'm around that size. Are you excited?

DRAUPADI. Yeah, I think I am.

HOLLY. Great! I think I have this super cute pink one that'll totally compliment your skin tone.

> *(As **HOLLY** leaves, the spotlight outside the shop lights up. **ALICE** is seen leaning against the sign breathing heavily. **MARIE** walks in sternly.)*

MARIE. What the fuck were you thinking talking to those ladies like that?

ALICE. I don't know mother; I don't know what the fuck I was thinking!

MARIE. You need to get your act together dear. What is wrong with you?

ALICE. Everything! Everything is wrong with me mom! My body is so fucking weird right now. There is something wrong with me!

MARIE. You and that tone of yours. You know, I have tried working with you on your behavior. Your father and I have given you too many chances. Skipping church, not learning your prayers. You haven't been active in your youth seminars like we talked about, and you've been forsaking your Bible studies. You have been skipping so many of your church duties, I can't even count them! Maybe we just need to keep you on a tighter leash.

ALICE. Whatever mother, I just need you to help me. I'm in deep shit. I'm –

MARIE. Of course, you're in deep shit sweetie. You used to be my beautiful daughter, so dutiful in her studies, and now, you dress like a slut and won't get up out of bed. Depression is no excuse for your irritating outbursts. Your father and I need to have a talk with you. Set you straight. Then I'll get my daughter back.

ALICE. *(Starts to cry.)* Mom! It's not about depression, mother, please. Listen to me! I need you to take me to the doctor. Someone who can help me.

MARIE. We will not be taking you to some doctor. Do you not know how disgraced our family would be if you were seen by a psychiatrist?

> (**MARIE** *starts walking towards* **ALICE**, *slowly, with* **ALICE** *slowly taking horrified steps backward.*)

I am your mother. You will follow my instructions, and I will help you the way I see fit.

ALICE. But you're not listening to me. *(She pauses.)* Mother I'm –

MARIE. Now, dear, we need to collect ourselves. Wipe your tears and fix your cardigan. It's slipping.

> (**MARIE** *seems to snap out of it.* **ALICE** *is very distraught, but she also tries to collect herself.*)

Ready to go inside Alice?

ALICE. Yes, mother. Just give me a second.

> (**MARIE** *leaves the outside of the shop and goes inside.*)

(To the audience.) Gift me all the time in the world.

> (*The spotlight fades on* **ALICE** *pulling out a pack of Marlboros. A spotlight lights on the dressing room, where* **SANVI** *is leaning against the wall.* **DRAUPADI** *is inside the dressing room. The audience can see her. She has her own bra on, and she is looking in the mirror.*)

SANVI. How do they feel Draupadi?

DRAUPADI. They feel awesome, *Amma*. I can't believe this, like I literally can't believe this!

SANVI. I think you should be thanking someone right about now. You know, for not letting you hop on a flight to go visit your *Amamma*.

DRAUPADI. Thanks Ma.

SANVI. You're welcome *Kanna*. I can't help but not want to spare you some pain.

DRAUPADI. Mother's duty and all?

SANVI. Yes. And no. We were too poor growing up. Your *Thatha* didn't have any money, and the little money he had, he didn't want to spend on me. When I started my period, I would have to wash my underwear and the lining cloth by hand. Every single day. It was terrible.

I can still smell it on my hands *Kanna*. The stench. I never wore pads till after I came to the United States. Even in Medical School, all the other girls had bras and camisoles. Your *Amamma* couldn't give me money to buy a bra. I was so self-conscious of my breasts and the clothes I wore. It was traumatic for me *Kanna*. But you have a better life. I don't want you to go through what I went through. I can make it better for you.

DRAUPADI. I'm so sorry. I can never understand how it was for you.

SANVI. You don't need to understand Draupadi. I never want you to understand what it felt like. I just want you to listen. Okay?

DRAUPADI. Always.

SANVI. Now how many do you want to take?

DRAUPADI. *(Putting on her shirt.)* Well, I really like these four. One sleeping bra, a t-shirt bra, this nice non-padded one, and a sports bra. Gosh, I can't wait to start running in these. Here I'll bring them out.

> *(DRAUPADI starts to gather the bras but she looks at the tag on one of them. It is very expensive. She sets them all down and looks at all the tags.)*

Actually, I think I'm okay. I'll only take the t-shirt bra.

SANVI. What's wrong Draupadi?

DRAUPADI. Nothing. It's just…I think it's too much to buy.

> *(SANVI goes inside the fitting room.)*

SANVI. Why? How much are they? Draupadi?

> *(DRAUPADI gives one of the bras to her mother. SANVI looks at the tag.)*

It's okay, *Kanna*, really.

DRAUPADI. It's not. This much for a bra? I don't need it that much. And besides, I can manage with the one I have.

SANVI. We can buy all of them. Really, it's okay. Let me do this for you.

DRAUPADI. I can't *Amma*. We need to spend this money on anything else. Literally anything else! We're already tight as it is.

SANVI. *(Takes the rest of the bras.)* We're not that tight. I can make this.

DRAUPADI. *(Grabbing the bras from **SANVI**.)* You don't need to do this for me.

SANVI. Stop it Draupadi. I am your mother. You must follow me on the decisions I make. I know what is best for you.

DRAUPADI. Fine, *mother*. You *can* make it. Just buy all of it, okay? *(To the audience.)* I promise, don't even care.

>   *(**DRAUPADI** storms out of the store and goes outside of the shop. The lights shift, and the spotlight turns on. **ALICE** blows a big puff of smoke, which **DRAUPADI** accidentally walks into, erupting into a fit of coughing.)*

What the actual fuck?

ALICE. I thought it would be funny.

DRAUPADI. It's not funny. It's illegal.

ALICE. You're illegal.

DRAUPADI. Well, you're immature.

ALICE. I'm a teenager. That's what we do. Immature shit.

DRAUPADI. Whatever.

>   *(A silent pause.)*

ALICE. What's my mother doing in there?

DRAUPADI. Trying on bras.

ALICE. What's your mother doing in there?

DRAUPADI. Buying bras.

ALICE. Bras, bras, bras. Those fucking bras. Fucking boobs. Fucking in general. It's the worst.

DRAUPADI. That's something we can agree on.

ALICE. *(Smiles.)* Want a drag?

DRAUPADI. Resorting to peer pressure now, are we?

ALICE. What? You're not a smoking virgin still. Are you?

DRAUPADI. Of course not. Just give it here.

> *(**ALICE** hands the cigarette to **DRAUPADI**. She takes a drag and blows out smoke rather smoothly. **ALICE** is deep in thought.)*

ALICE. I'm...not a virgin anymore.

DRAUPADI. Congrats.

ALICE. I'm pregnant.

DRAUPADI. *(Blows out another puff.)* Double Congrats.

> *(**DRAUPADI** pauses. She then realizes what **ALICE** just said.)*

Wait. What?

ALICE. A little alien is growing inside me. Cute, isn't it?

DRAUPADI. Wow. You really shouldn't be smoking.

ALICE. *(Snickers, with no happiness.)* My body is going to grow. My boobs are going to be even larger than that lady's. They're gonna be larger than fucking balloons.

DRAUPADI. That's not a bad thing you know. Boobs grow.

ALICE. Right. You said that already.

DRAUPADI. That's what happened to my boobs.

ALICE. You were pregnant?

DRAUPADI. No! I was puberty – er, I was pubertal. My breasts grew pretty large in a short time. By the time I was eleven, I was around a 32C.

ALICE. I'm a 32C.

DRAUPADI. Exactly. I was terrified. Being so young and having that was hard. Kids teased me. I couldn't wear anything without feeling like I was baring my entire body to everyone. My self esteem sucked. On top of that, my boobs just kept growing, and I could never find a comfortable bra. Turns out I'm actually a 28G, which is so fucking weird. I didn't even know a size like that existed.

ALICE. It's not a bad size actually. Small frame, big boobs. Every guy's fantasy, right?

DRAUPADI. It's not about the guy. It's never about the guy. I can barely support the weight of my chest. I run track, but I can't run because all I feel is pain.

ALICE. Well, you're here now. The Candyland for bras.

DRAUPADI. But they're so expensive. My family is already sorta spread. My parents had to go through so much in India, and my life is nothing in comparison. I can't be another burden to them by spending money so flagrantly. Even if my Ma's okay with it, It'd still be selfish.

ALICE. If she's trying to do a nice thing for you, you should let her.

DRAUPADI. I don't want her to do nice things for me. I just want her to know that I can help her and take on some responsibility. One bra is sixty dollars. How can I do that to her?

ALICE. Isn't that fucked up? A place like this that thrives on inclusivity, is actually not inclusive? How ironic. They have every size beholden to mankind, but it's only for the super-fucking-high echelon of people. You have to be well-off to buy these.

DRAUPADI. Exactly. Other bra shops have limited bras, but they're affordable. The bras that actually fit and feel good? Expensive. How does that even work? Victoria Secret bra fitters literally lie so that you can buy their bras, and they get to take your money. But places like this...they fit. They feel great; they are heaven! But the ticket to heaven is so fucking expensive.

(By this point, the girls are somewhat buzzed.)

ALICE. You could get surgery. I had a friend. Hated her boobs, so she got a breast reduction.

DRAUPADI. My Ma wanted me to. After we went to like, a gazillion stores to no avail, she brought it up since she knew a good doctor. And I hate it. It's expensive, still. I would never afford it. You said something before – the "super-fucking-high echelon of people." That's who plastic surgery is for, you know, unless you go to Tijuana to have concrete injected up your ass.

ALICE. And what if it went wrong? Like, your tits could turn into a uni-boob or something. You never know.

DRAUPADI. Totally. By that point, I just had to understand that the world revolves around making people feel like shit; money is exclusivity. The only way you're gonna make bank is if you make people conform. Thing is, boobs like mine exist! Society needs to understand that they are alienating a whole demographic of women that feel unwanted because of their standards. Because of their greed for money!

ALICE. Yeah! Fuck them! What gives them the right to make you into some sort of...anomaly? They don't have shit. It's their fault. You have a normal body. You're not inferior just because you're not the representative. The representative isn't even the majority. It's the rich!

DRAUPADI. Truth.

(**ALICE** *lights another cigarette, and they both take a drag. The smoke clouds the stage.*)

What about your little alien? Have you told your mom?

ALICE. *(Scoffs.)* Hell no. She thinks I'm depressed which is right up there along with the seven deadly sins. The second I do tell her, I'd be out onto the streets. My father would disown me. My parents and I..."getting along" is not entirely accurate, but we make do. I'm too young to lose the only support I have. I would be alone. I would be a disgrace, I would wither. I would have no one.

DRAUPADI. That's not true. You have friends. You have people that could help. Multiple support systems you could call on.

ALICE. No, I don't. God I hate it when people say that, as if it'll all be okay, as if you know what I'm going through! All my "friends" are churchies. "Praise the lord" and all that shit. I grew up into it, but it's not really my thing. I honestly felt chaffed by it. Uber-religious parents like mine seriously chock my style. And I guess I wasn't all that *mature*, when dealing with *confusions* about my religious beliefs. I can admit that I put my parents through a ringer. Hell, I thought losing my virginity would be the greatest fuck you to God, but lo and behold, the guy had an Uno reverse card stuck in his back pocket. I guess he had the last word.

DRAUPADI. The guy always has the last word, but you can still choose what you want to do with your pregnancy. Do you want the baby?

ALICE. No.

DRAUPADI. Then there are options for that. You could do adoption. That way you don't keep the kid –

ALICE. Stop right there. This thing ain't a kid. It's a little alien. Okay? It's a whisp of air, a non-existent ant, a little termite-thing eating my uterus alive. Got it?

DRAUPADI. That's...fair. What about abortion?

ALICE. Haven't you heard? Abortion is a sin. It's the devil's work.

DRAUPADI. Do you, like, really believe that?

ALICE. *(Scoffs.)* No.

DRAUPADI. Planned Parenthood could help? They can be on the down low. Pretty discrete. There are so many safe abortion options – the abortion pill, which causes something close to a miscarriage. In-clinic abortions are also a consideration. How many weeks are you?

ALICE. Nine weeks. I think.

DRAUPADI. Thank God were not in Texas.

ALICE. Fuck God. If he was actually looking over us through his uppity seat, he wouldn't have let that pass.

DRAUPADI. Yeah. True.

(They take another drag.)

ALICE. It's not like having a baby is a bad thing. It's a wonderful thing. I think. But I'm a teenager. I want to do my immature shit. Hell, I did my immature shit and look where I'm at now. A devout Christian girl knocked up to the gods. I just can't have this baby. I don't want my body to change right now. I want to stay how I am!

DRAUPADI. Having the baby won't change you. You'll always be Alice. Even if your body changes, you'll always be whatever you are inside. Even if that's Atheist-Alice.

ALICE. I know that. But I'm not ready for...that. It's my decision to not have this child. Society needs to respect it! Folks can have different bodies and different boobs. People need to accept that I don't want to have this child, and that I can do whatever I want with whatever is under my skin. I'm not hurting anybody; it's not political. It's my life! It's my whole life in front of me, and I'm staring at the abyss as this confused teenager, and I want to hug it.

> (**DRAUPADI** *rubs* **ALICE***'s shoulder, and* **ALICE** *closes her eyes.*)

We're not anomalies. We exist right?

DRAUPADI. Yeah, we do.

> (*The teens hold hands and look at each other.*)

You know, if you need somebody to take you to the clinic, and, you know, pick you up, I can give you my number? I mean, I'm basically free whenever, and you can just give me a call and tell me you need me –

> (**ALICE** *drops her cigarette and envelops* **DRAUPADI** *in a hug.*)

ALICE. Thank you. Thank you for listening to me.

> (**DRAUPADI** *hugs* **ALICE** *back.*)

DRAUPADI. Always. Always.

> (*The spotlight fades on the two girls hugging. It lingers for a few seconds on the "Under My Skin" sign. The stage lights again, and the audience finds* **DRAUPADI** *on the couch. Her eyes are closed and she is inactive. The bra shop is bathed in an unnerving light. The* **PREGNANT WOMAN** *enters on one side of the stage.*)

PREGNANT WOMAN. Once upon a time there was a princess named DRAUPADI.

> (**DRAUPADI**'s eyes open and her body is activated.)

She was born from a powerful hearth.

> (**SANVI** enters the stage and hugs **DRAUPADI**)

She had the purest, darkest skin that was likened to the beautiful god Krishna, foretold to become Queen in her own right. And yet, the fortunes gambled against her, thrusting her into the clutches of the world.

> (The **MEN** appear, one on either side of the stage, pushing **SANVI** aside, and grabbing each of **DRAUPADI**'s arms. She is screaming, but a loud rumbling drowns her out.)

The World had taken her life away. Her bonds were to be revoked, her exterior to be stripped and shed at her feet.

> (A spotlight shines on **MARIE** and **ALICE**. **ALICE** is in her blue dress, her cardigan at her feet. **MARIE** takes the cardigan and forcefully puts it on **ALICE**. the **MEN** try to strip **DRAUPADI**.)

DRAUPADI & ALICE. I don't belong to you. Someone help me!

> (A long red sari flies in above both **DRAUPADI** and **ALICE**, one for each of them. They release themselves from their respective holds and wrap their bodies in the fabric.)

PREGNANT WOMAN. Krishna listened. The sari keeps descending. It never stops, never leaves. On that day, it protected her modesty, gifting her warmth that the world so severely lacked.

> (**SANVI** *finally approaches* **ALICE** *and kisses her forehead.* **MARIE** *exits the stage.* **SANVI** *walks to* **DRAUPADI** *and hugs her, kissing her forehead. The* **MEN** *drop* **DRAUPADI***'s arms and exit.*)

PREGNANT WOMAN. At the other end of the sari, was something Draupadi never expected. Friendship.

> (**SANVI** *stands in the middle of the stage. The girls reconvene next to her, facing each other on either side of* **SANVI**.)

A friendship she never thought she ever needed.

> (**PREGNANT WOMAN** *exits. Lights return to normal.*)

SANVI. I know I am not your mother Alice, but I'm so happy that you decided to tell an adult. We'll try and help you out, okay?

ALICE. I think I'm going to throw up.

SANVI. That's okay too. It's okay to feel whatever you're feeling.

DRAUPADI. I told you this was a good idea. I knew you could help Ma.

ALICE. Thank you. Thank you so much! I don't know what I could ever do to pay you back.

SANVI. I just listened honey. That's the minimum. We adults have a duty to our children.

ALICE. But I just met you.

SANVI. I "just met" a lot of adults when I was young, Alice. Not one of them helped me. Maybe if they had, I would have been spared the pain. Maybe, giving you that can make up for what I never got. Besides, I'm just amazed that my Draupadi made a friend!

DRAUPADI. I can make friends Ma. I'm not antisocial.

ALICE. Please. If I hadn't gotten to you, you would have been a goner.

SANVI. *(Laughs.)* I think I like this one, *kanna*. I think I really like this one.

DRAUPADI. Can you just leave Ma?

> (**SANVI** *laughs and leaves for the cash register.* **HOLLY** *is there as well.*)

ALICE. I think I'm going to talk to her.

DRAUPADI. You don't have to.

ALICE. I want to. Is it weird that I want to be honest with her, even though I know I'm going to get hurt?

DRAUPADI. Of course you still have hope. You're her daughter, Alice. You will always hold out hope for her.

ALICE. I just want her to love me.

DRAUPADI. She does love you, just in her own way. The people we love don't always do the right things for us.

ALICE. And you'll be there? If shit hits the fan?

DRAUPADI. Always.

ALICE. Okay.

> *(The girls stare at each other. A smile starts to spread on both of their faces.)*

DRAUPADI & ALICE. Okay.

> *(The girls grin at each other.)*

ALICE. Give your mother a break. She's lovely. And tell her thanks. Again.

DRAUPADI. I will. And you'll call me?

ALICE. I will.

(The girls hold hands and hug. ALICE walks to the door. She stares at DRAUPADI, who waves at her. ALICE turns towards to door, takes a breath, and exits the stage. A doorbell can be heard as she exits. SANVI joins DRAUPADI and hands her the bag of bras.)

DRAUPADI. Amma...

SANVI. I know you think that this is a lot, but it isn't. Like I told your new friend, I have a duty to my children. To you. My daughter. I love you, and I want to give you what I could never have as a child. Can you accept this bag, not as a necessity, but as a gift?

DRAUPADI. But what about the money? What are we going to do?

SANVI. We'll figure it out my *kanna*. Together.

*(**SANVI** offers **DRAUPADI** her hand. **DRAUPADI** takes it, and they exit the stage. The stage lights fade to black.)*

The End

www.ingramcontent.com/pod-product-compliance
Lightning Source LLC
Chambersburg PA
CBHW072005290426
44109CB00018B/2139